DR. JACQUELINE LANDRU

"The WHY NOT? Challenge"

SAY "YES!" TO SUCCESS WITH SCHOOL-COMMUNITY PARTNERSHIPS

SCHOLASTIC

Dad, I dedicate this book to you.

You are the epitome of community empowerment! You are never afraid to smile and light up a room. You taught me about love for life, love for people, and love for community. Your sparkle will never go out and will continue to be a light along my path. You are my hero!

Acknowledgments

I wish to acknowledge my parents, Earline and Willie Landrum, whose support, love, and example gave me the confidence I needed to continue. They taught me about faith. I want to thank my sister, Catherine, nephew Ryan, and extended family members who constantly inspire me to keep striving to be my best and to laugh often. I want to thank my wonderful husband, Aaron, and my son, Scott, for supporting me along this journey and encouraging me every step of the way. I am indebted to my Scholastic literary team, Karen Baicker, Danny Miller, and Dr. Lois Bridges, who closely guided me throughout the writing and research of this project and helped me realize the power of storytelling. Finally, I honor and esteem Greg Worrell, president of Scholastic Education, who believed in me and my "Why not?" message from the beginning. I am eternally grateful to each of you.

Scholastic is not responsible for the content of third-party websites and does not endorse any site or imply that the information on the site is error-free, correct, accurate, or reliable.

Photos ©: 4 top left, 9: mattjeacock/Getty Images; 7, 21, 47, 67, and 97: Kerry James; 23, 27, 31, 33, 41, 42, 45, 60, 69, 78, 91, 92, 102, and 105: Courtesty of Dr. Jacqueline L. Sanderlin; All other photos © Shutterstock.com

Publisher: Karen Baicker
Content Editor: Lois Bridges
Developmental Editor: Danny Miller
Editorial director: Sarah Longhi
Art director: Liana Zamora
Interior designer: Maria Lilja

Contents

INTRODUCTION

All Children Deserve a Why Not? Approach

As I reflect on my life, I realize why I have truly embraced the words, "Why not?" My mother, Mrs. Earline Landrum, was a nurse by occupation and a strong and uncompromising parent by nature. She is a woman who never backed down when it came to her children. Whenever she saw a wall, she tried to find out how to scale it. Even today, I think she actually looks for problems to fix. That is my mother. She has a way with people that is almost unbelievable. Over the years, I have seen her do some pretty amazing things for me and my sister, Cathy. She secured thousands of dollars from financial sponsors to support me when I was competing in beauty pageants, hired the best tutors for us even when her funds were low, and even took on the U.S. Department of Veterans Affairs in a 14-year battle to get our dad the benefits that were due him. She is a force to be reckoned with.

It was my parents who first planted the "Why Not?" idea in their children's heads. I never knew where it would take me, but I was listening.

When my sister and I were in elementary school, our mother was determined to enroll us in a school that she felt would provide us with a better education than our neighborhood school. While we lived in a nice middle-class community, the other school was in a more exclusive neighborhood and had a lot more resources and programs.

My mother believed that this other school would be more challenging for us with all of its additional enrichment opportunities. She believed in diversity as well, and yet this school was not diverse—it was 100% Caucasian.

In fact, if we were accepted into the school, we would be the first two black students they ever enrolled. But the truth was that our current school was not diverse either. It was made up almost entirely of African American students and our parents wanted us to also be exposed to other cultures. Our father had traveled the world while in the Navy and had met many different people. He taught himself Spanish and could speak it fluently. He cooked us foods from different cultures and wanted us exposed to every race. My parents felt that attending this other school would broaden our minds.

Once she found out about it, the school stayed in my mother's heart. On her lunch breaks, she used to walk around the exterior of the school and drive around the community. She loved the flowers, the trees, and the green grass in front of almost everyone's home.

66 I decided to ask them to tell me what would make our school even better. I told them to imagine anything they wanted and yell it out! 99

Our parents discussed the pros and cons of us attending this school and knew there would be some hurdles they would have to get through to get us enrolled. It was already the middle of the school year and we did not have a permit to attend the school; it definitely did not seem like the right time for us to transfer. One night, my sister and I overheard our parents talking in the living room. My mother leaned over to our dad and said, "Why not? At least I can try. Maybe they will welcome our girls. They are good girls." When I heard her say that, I smiled with pride.

The following morning, she drove to our new school. She walked in with her beautiful smile and asked to speak to the principal. Because of the permit issue, he was hesitant. Then she pivoted and asked if she could stay and help that day. She told him that she took the day off and she loved to volunteer. He allowed her to help on the yard, in the library, and to monitor the lunch line. It was a different world back then—today, she would have had to submit fingerprints and get approved as a school volunteer. Back then, they just trusted her smile and her enthusiasm. My mother was able to meet the teachers and the staff and became friendly with them. I think my mom was working her magic.

Before the end of the day, the principal came and thanked her for taking time to volunteer at a school at which her children were not enrolled. She told him she was happy to do it. In fact, she did such a great job that several people on the staff had told her that they wanted her to stay. Well, to her surprise, the principal did, too. And he wanted her to bring her daughters with her next time. That principal ended up helping my mother get the permit we needed and we soon enrolled in their school.

My sister and I never forgot that day. In fact, I believe those foundational years were the catalyst that created the Why Not? mindset I have today.

Years later, when I was a principal in Compton, California, I was on the playground during one of my morning assemblies with my scholars. (I always called my students scholars because I felt that it was important for me to hold them to that expectation. That's the term I will use throughout this book.) Many came from tough circumstances and it was important to remind them of their potential. I ran school assemblies nearly every morning on our playground, mainly to give the teachers time to prepare for class, but also to pep up the kids for the day. We would repeat a multitude of affirmations, chants, and songs. Sometimes, if I was in a particularly good mood, we might even dance! Morning assemblies were always an exciting time for me because I had a chance to speak to all of our students at the same time. But this one morning was different.

The question, "Why not?" opens up doors of possibilities. Think about it!

Instead of repeating the same things as we usually did, I decided to ask them to tell me what would make our school even better. I told them to imagine anything they wanted and yell it out!

Many of them literally stared back at me like I took them by surprise. But when I continued to nudge them, they began spouting out answers like new basketball courts, musical instruments, field trips, and much more. Once they got on a roll, I could hardly stop them! Finally, one of them shouted, "Can we really get all this stuff, Dr. Sanderlin?" I thought about it and yelled back, "Why not?" And that was it!

Hearing myself say "Why not?", it was like I lit a fuse that would not burn out. All of them began shouting those words in unison. "Why not? Why not? Why not?" Soon the parents and the staff joined in. "Why not?

Why not? Why not?" I could not stop them. It was almost like the words created an energy that could not be contained.

As I walked around the campus or visited classrooms, every scholar would say, "Why not?" I knew there was something to this Why Not? business when one of my parents made a T-shirt for me with the phrase "Why Not?" graced on the front. Something was happening at my school and it wasn't just a passing fad. Those words became our school mantra. Little did we know that this simple question would spark a flame of community empowerment and partnerships.

About This Book

This book is divided into two parts. The first part focuses on getting ready for successful partnerships. I am convinced that before real partnerships can come, you have to empower your community to get on board. This first half of the book will help prepare and position your school for developing all types of powerful community partnerships. I am convinced that school leaders should focus on community empowerment before attempting to develop community partnerships in order to create a sustainable impact for their scholars and school.

Please go to **scholastic.com/ WhyNotResources** for additional checklists, forms, and other materials that will help you with your personal Why Not? Challenge.

The second part of the book provides strategies to help you create and maintain successful partnerships. To be clear, I am specifically focused on philanthropic partnerships that often come through businesses, corporations, CEOs, and individuals who have a strong desire to support education.

Each chapter includes action steps and personal stories designed to help you take the Why Not? Challenge and make a difference in your school and community. The personal stories included are lessons I have learned over the years that I hope assist you with empowering your school community and developing sustainable partnerships.

PART I
Preparing for Successful School-Community Partnerships

Before developing successful partnerships, it's important to empower your community and get them enrolled in the idea of powerful partnerships. When I reflect on my early experiences with partnerships, I realize that I was too focused on my school's many needs. My desire for partnerships was focused on superficial short-term fixes. I was not thinking about sustainability at all.

When I thought of developing partnerships, I only wanted partners to help us or write us a check that went beyond my school budget. I didn't have time (I thought) to empower my community. I needed new stuff for my school by any means necessary and for good reasons since I was in an under-resourced community. I had a large population of troubled youth who came from complicated situations like foster homes, homelessness, and group homes. I believe they deserved better!

"Here is the ultimate truth that I learned: If you don't empower your community, nothing will happen. Empower means to give someone the authority or power to do something."

That was not the right approach and it did not produce the outcomes I hoped for. Yes, we would get a few donations, but never any lasting partnerships.

Here is the ultimate truth that I learned: If you don't empower your community, nothing will happen. *Empower* means to give someone the authority or power to do something. As educational leaders, we have the power to get our local community members (families, businesses, corporations, CEOs, politicians, etc.) excited about our school vision and mission! Why not?

Don't be afraid to do this. In fact, I think it is our obligation to do it. Our scholars are depending on us. Our parents are depending on us. Our community is depending on us! So how do you empower your community? It all starts with a shift!

Shifting from Engagement to Empowerment

I want you to consider a shift from engaging your community to empowering your community. For me, these are two very different approaches. Let's face it, we, as educators, have been discussing community engagement for years, which basically means creating opportunities for involvement. Involvement is a wonderful thing, but I think it's time to take that to another level.

Think of it like this: When we engage, it is like getting a lease. When we empower, it is ownership! See the difference? When we empower our community, we are offering an opportunity to share in ownership. And ownership, my friend, translates into investment.

66 When we engage, it is like getting a lease. When we empower, it is ownership! 99

An Unlikely Example of Empowerment

At one time, I was the principal of a school adjacent to a park where gang members would regularly meet up with one another. Our scholars would watch them through our chain-link fence as they were having their meetings. It was not a positive sight. We would often hear loud cursing and fighting, and we'd often witness police activity. Every loud sound would cause us to look over and duck. It was dangerous. I thought, this is not what young students should be exposed to.

I made an executive decision, against the advice of my staff, to go over and ask these gang members if they would consider holding their meetings somewhere else. On my way there, I was becoming less and less confident. As I approached their circle, they looked at me with curiosity. They must have thought I had lost my mind. As I was asking, I began to think about what I was actually doing. I had the gall to ask them to leave their community park where they grew up, played, and now had their gang meetings. I only worked in the neighborhood and

I went home every day. My actions were to disempower them—not empower them. To this day, I am so glad that I had that realization in that moment. My plan instantly shifted before the conversation went south.

On the spur of the moment, I decided to ask them if they would be willing to come speak to my male students in a new afterschool program called Gentleman Scholars. From that point on, their faces changed from confused and irritated to possibly interested. I explained the mission was to help them with etiquette skills and positive behaviors. One of the gang leaders spoke up and said, "I like that. Yeah, we could do that. What do you want us to do?" Another said, "I used to go to your school and we didn't have that when I was there—good idea." I can honestly say, I initially didn't know what I wanted them to do. I just knew this was one way to get them out of the park...but on my campus?

The next day, I was on my way to work and drove past a restaurant called Three Bears Burgers. I was drawn to the restaurant because I could smell the grilled burgers a mile away. I thought that it would be great to order food for the upcoming Gentleman Scholars meeting. I shared this with the manager who happened to take my order. She became so excited that she was willing to donate all the burgers for that day. I was shocked!

What happened next still amazes me when I think about it. This woman decided to bring her team and cook the burgers and the fries at the meeting! It was at that moment when I realized that she had become empowered by the idea of participating in this community event. She told me that she grew up in the same neighborhood and her family had gone through many challenges. By then she was catering major events in Hollywood, but she felt that this was an opportunity to help out in a way that was important to her.

On the day of the meeting, the gang members came in smiling because they smelled the burgers as they entered the school. While my young Gentleman Scholars ate, they listened intently to each gang member as they shared their different stories. Each one had a different path and some surprising turns. While some came from broken homes, others grew up with both parents and finished high school, yet they became members of the gang in order to survive where they lived. As we listened, they all talked about how not to get into gangs. They gave advice and said if they could do it again, they would have done it differently. This was the first and most powerful meeting we had to kick off the Gentlemen Scholars program. They brought something I could not...they brought community empowerment. If I could do it over again, I would not change a thing.

After hearing their stories, there was not a dry eye in the room. I learned so much that day. Instead of asking these young men to leave their community, I now invited them to be empowered to help their community. While I thought this was the end, it was only the beginning. The park became a passion project for all of us to clean up. The entire community got involved! We painted murals, remodeled the community pool, and made it a place for families to feel safe to go to. It became an oasis instead of an eyesore. More than that, it became a vehicle for community empowerment.

The Gentleman Scholars program lasted for many years, continuing to bring in guest speakers, field trips, events, and new experiences. We even had alumni come back and share their stories.

This is certainly one way to empower your community—inviting them to share their stories and to work with you. Think about your local community and find avenues and pathways to work together, collaboratively. The empowerment will be like a ripple effect.

From that day forward, I continued to develop a Why Not? mindset and to believe anything was possible for my school. I started thinking big and dreaming even bigger. I got bitten by the Why Not? bug!

> **66** *Think about your local community and find avenues and pathways to work together, collaboratively. The empowerment will be like a ripple effect.* **99**

Develop a Why Not? Mindset

Before I began to empower my community, I had to truly believe that we had something to be empowered about. It was not enough to get people excited, it had to be much more than that. We all had to fully realize our value in the community.

It was a new state of mind that we had to adopt, and it wasn't always easy. Listen, when you have such a high percentage of your scholars in foster homes or homeless, and many other challenges, it is easy

to take on a negative mindset or at least a less optimistic one. What I didn't realize was that my mindset was trickling down to my teachers, staff, scholars, and parents. In fact, it was going out into our community.

So, if I was going to empower my community, I had to change from a fixed mindset to a Why Not? growth mindset. "In the fixed mindset, everything is about the outcome. If you fail—or if you're not the best—it's all been wasted. The growth mindset allows people to value what they're doing regardless of the outcome" (Dweck, 2006).

Once I began to change my attitude, I had the idea of partnering with a college that was located across the street from my school. It seemed like a great idea and a wonderful opportunity for our youth. I was not sure of the logistics, but I knew we needed to make a connection. Then one night I had a strange but vivid dream where I saw a bridge that connected our school to the college. The next morning, I woke up and had no idea what to make of my dream, but I got up the courage to call the president of the college. To my surprise, I was able to get him on the phone and tell him about my dream. I was shocked when he told me that he had always wanted to partner with our school and build a "pipeline" from kindergarten to college.

> **66** *If I was going to empower my community, I had to change from a fixed mindset to a Why Not? growth mindset.* **99**

We talked about it for hours. We talked about all the positive possibilities like mentoring, tutoring, and enrichment programs that they could help with. We were both coming from a Why Not? mindset. We didn't know exactly how the partnership would work or whether it was feasible, but we both ended up saying, "Why not?" Let me stop here and tell you that you don't need to know how all the time. All you need to have is a Why Not? drive and the rest will take care of itself.

We knew we could not do this alone. We had to empower our local community of parents, business owners, church leaders, school board members, scholars, and other stakeholders. After months of collaboration, community meetings, board meetings, and other input, we ultimately created a kindergarten-through-college pipeline! Our local community and families had an accessible pathway to college for their children that did not exist before. Before we knew it, our local community became involved and soon everyone was empowered to help this vision come to life.

> **"** *A big part of empowering your community is sharing your dream. They need to know what you are thinking about. By sharing, you are inviting people to listen.* **"**

It was a huge success! We created additional tutoring programs, mentoring programs, Saturday Science programs, and a variety of other innovative enrichment programs. It was a dream come true! And I I truly believe this all happened because we had developed a Why Not? mindset.

As you set out to empower your community, be willing to think outside the box. If you are going to bring change to the community through your school, then your community needs you to have a Why Not? mindset. When you do, you will find so many people who were just waiting for that idea, spark, or motivation.

A big part of empowering your community is sharing your dream. They need to know what you are thinking about. What if I never told the president of the community college about my dream? What if we didn't believe in the possibilities? While you are waiting for your community to come around and support your scholars, your community is waiting on you!

I know everyone has their ideas of whether leaders are born or developed. I think it's both. As school leaders, it is in our nature to empower others, but we also need to learn how to do it effectively. Let's look at some action steps below that can help you develop or grow your Why Not? mindset.

Action Steps for Developing a Why Not? Mindset

1 Dream Possibilities

Developing a Why Not? mindset requires us to dream big.
Your ability to think this way can empower your community in a monumental way. Let's examine the word *possibility*. A possibility is something that may actually happen. In other words, there is a likelihood, probability, or prospect that what you want may occur. Isn't your school worth your ability to dream possibilities? Sure it is!

I do realize the incredibly busy job of an administrator. You might be saying to yourself, "I don't dream that big" or "I am burned out." If that is the case, this is a great time to do a mindset overhaul and incubate. Think about hitting the reset button and let your dreams soar. Believe me, your ability to dream possibilities will empower your community who are just waiting to be inspired. Don't get sidetracked with trying to figure out how to make your dreams come true. *How* is none of your business! Just focus and keep your mind on your Why Not? and the rest will come. You don't have to go it alone either. That is what a community is for. They want to help and are waiting to be asked. Think about all the businesses that surround your school or the ones you drive by each day. In one way or another, they probably have ideas on how to better the community as well.

Think bigger! Think about your school being the solution to the success of the community. Think about your school being the vehicle of change to educate new leaders to take on the world. I dare you to take on a Why Not? mindset and watch what happens. When you start to think like that, it changes your perception about your own school and puts you in the driver's seat. But you need copilots, and those copilots are your community. When you take on a Why Not? mindset, it has the ability to attract like-minded people. Everyone in your community will not think like you. Some will need to be convinced, influenced, or challenged to think differently. That is your community empowerment challenge.

Don't let a quiet community fool you. If they appear disengaged or uninvolved, this might be because no one empowered them to act! Let that person be you. Talk to them, listen to them, and create opportunities for dialogue. Each of those will help mold and shape thoughts, beliefs, and attitudes. What I am talking about is your community culture. It starts in the mind. What are you thinking about?

2 Create Possibility Boards

This exercise will get your community to imagine again.
I invited all the local businesses with a flyer explaining what we were doing. And many of them showed up! We also had food, which was another hook. I honestly think that some people in the local business community enjoyed opportunities to get away from work. Whatever their motivations are is okay!

Each person used different things to create his or her ideas. Some used pictures about putting in a pool and others used grass to show we needed more grass. Whether we would actually get those things or not, this activity was a vehicle to help us think about possibilities, which is a necessary first step for community empowerment. We displayed the possibility boards around the school, which became another conversation starter for those who looked at them. Many in the community were proud of what they did. This activity helped them think about solutions, rather than all the problems. It helped refocus them on being solution-oriented and not problem-oriented.

Think about this as an opportunity for your community to meet and talk. There are so many ways to empower our communities and have fun at the same time.

3 Lead a School-Community Walk

One surefire way to empower your community and heighten the Why Not? mindset with everyone involved is to have a community walk! One year, I really wanted to get my community more involved and empowered, as well as change the negative mindset about our school. Our school had a bad reputation because of where it was located, and this was hard to change.

We took time to go out into the community and we invited all the local stores, companies, organizations, and residents to walk with us on a specific day. Hundreds of people came out! The highlight of the day was when a local motorcycle group joined in and rode beside us. We all loved it! They blasted music, spread out, and rode alongside us. This helped protect us as we walked.

All 600 of us marched around the block. We sure caused a stir in the community! Everyone stopped and pulled over, clapped as we went by, and smiles were everywhere. It was sheer community empowerment! As we continued this tradition each year, we watched the mindset of various community members change over time. We gave them something positive to talk about.

Try a school-community walk and watch the empowerment take shape. If you do this, be ready for your community to be all hands on deck. That is what you want. An empowered community that will help your school, protect your school and scholars, and uphold your school mission. That is what a community is for. When they realize you didn't forget them and you included them, they will do the same for you. So, try it—your community will like it.

4 Throw a Back-to-School Pep Rally

While it is important for you to have a Why Not? mindset, the same is true for your school and community. Sometimes it is easier to work on oneself, but an entire community can be a bit daunting.

I enjoyed holding a back-to-school pep rally each year. The purpose was to start the new school year with a bang while empowering the local community. I was always astonished at how many parents and community members would come out. It was a very festive event. We invited the entire community. We had plenty of food, balloons, a stage, decorations, and, of course, music. Every class would come out and participate in this school-wide event. The students would make posters with positive quotes and march around in a big circle. The rally caused a lot of hype and school pride, not only for the scholars, but for our parents and the local community.

Action Steps

Acknowledgment and praise are priceless, especially when it is authentic and made public. Rallies make a fine opportunity for you to deepen the Why Not? mindset within your community, recognize achievements, share upcoming events, honor individuals and businesses, promote positive thinking, develop a common language, create teamwork, and position your school community to be empowered.

You may already be doing something like this but have not reached out to invite your local community to come and celebrate with you. Now is the time! In my opinion, every school should do this. Rallies like this stir up hope and optimism, and can change mindsets.

The bottom line is to do something exciting and new, whether that is a fun community event like a community carnival, community picnic, community walk, or a back-to-school pep rally. Just do it! As the saying goes, build it and they will come.

5 Know Your Value

It is easier to have confidence, empower your community, and have a Why Not? mindset when you know your school's value. Please realize that your school adds value to the community. Your school matters—a lot! This is incredibly important because sometimes we need to be reminded of just how important our schools are to our communities. What value does your school add? Well, to start, you are educating the next generation of employees, CEOs, and future leaders.

When you know that, you can use those points of light and common language to speak about your school and share your value to help expand your community with the programs it offers. What you think about your school is essential for jumpstarting community empowerment. Share your school's value with all the business leaders you know. Success breeds success, so think like a business leader. The community needs to be reminded of just how important your school is.

Developing a Why Not? mindset is a process. It is realizing your school is worth the effort of empowering your community to make lasting change for your scholars. It is something we must do as school leaders for sustainable impact. Once we believe our school deserves the best, we will never settle for less. Believe in possibilities because you expect great things to happen!

 FURTHERING THE CONVERSATION

Mindset: The New Psychology of Success
by Carol S. Dweck

After decades of research, world-renowned Stanford University psychologist Carol S. Dweck, PhD, discovered a simple but groundbreaking idea: the power of mindset. In this brilliant book, she shows how success in school, work, sports, the arts, and almost every area of human endeavor can be dramatically influenced by how we think about our talents and abilities. People with a *fixed mindset*—those who believe that abilities are fixed—are less likely to flourish than those with a *growth mindset*—those who believe that abilities can be developed. *Mindset* reveals how great parents, teachers, managers, and athletes can put this idea to use to foster outstanding accomplishment.

Dweck also introduces a phenomenon she calls false growth mindset and guides people toward adopting a deeper, truer growth mindset. She also expands the mindset concept beyond the individual, applying it to the cultures of groups and organizations. With the right mindset, you can motivate those you lead, teach, and love—to transform their lives and your own.

Take the Why Not? Challenge: Make a Possibility Board!

Now it is time to take that dream and make your school possibility board. Invite your local community leaders to come and add their thoughts, ideas, pictures, and dreams! Start off with a long piece of butcher paper so there will be enough room for everyone to write on it. This will also make it more collaborative and fun. You can get more sophisticated and use canvases, charts, etc.

Go to a local arts and crafts store and buy markers, watercolors, paintbrushes, stickers, magazines, and more. In fact, if you tell the store manager what you are doing, they might even donate the materials to help support your efforts. While you are at it, invite the store manager to come visit your school, too! Don't forget to get food. That is a sure way to get everyone there and it makes for a happy and productive day!

REFLECTION PROMPTS

- **How has your mindset changed, if at all?**
- **What dreams do you want to be turned into possibilities?**
- **Which business will you ask to be on your leadership team?**
- **When is a good time for you to have a Dream Fest or school pep rally?**

Why Not? Challenge #2
Embrace Your Community

When I was a principal, I remember going to work and then straight home each night, rarely ever making stops along the way. One day, because I worked very late that day, I decided to do some quick grocery shopping at a store near the school.

As I was gathering items in my basket, I heard a voice say, "Look, there's Dr. Sanderlin!" I looked back and saw it was one of my third-grade scholars. She was tugging on her mother and pointing

at me. Her eyes glared and she had a huge smile. She then said, "What are you doing here?" I told her I was shopping for food and I didn't live at the school. Her mother chuckled. She wondered why I was there at all. As I went up and down each aisle with my basket, they kept following me and peering down each corner. They were literally in disbelief that I shopped at "their" market.

This taught me a valuable lesson. I wanted to empower my community with activities and events, but I had never embraced it. When you embrace a community, you take time to visit the places, dine there, play there, and maybe even visit some of the places of worship there. Take time to get to know the real people in the area around your school and the connection to the community will go both ways.

> **66** *Take time to get to know the real people in the area around your school and the connection to the community will go both ways.* **99**

Embracing Your Internal School Community

The internal school community are all the people in your building (teachers, staff, scholars, volunteers, and so on). Sometimes we can forget about the people we see every day, but they matter a lot. They have ideas, thoughts, and suggestions to offer, too! They need to know we value them and that we genuinely care.

One day, I went to my PTA meeting. In lieu of our regular meeting, we had food, played music, and just talked. We got to know each other better and had such a great morning. It was just what we needed! I took time to sit with each parent and hear some of their stories. We hugged, embraced, and even shed a few tears. It was just what the doctor ordered.

The next day, one of the parents from the meeting brought in a check for $5,000. She told me she was moved by our time together and wanted to invest in her child's school. She felt empowered.

I learned a valuable lesson that day. I could not forget the people in my internal school community or take them for granted. After that day, I began to embrace the internal community even more. When I did, great things happened. I developed a team of scholars to work and keep our school garden up. Then their families came and it turned into what we called Foster Farmers. They made the garden lovely, and I didn't have to remind them. One of my teachers built our first Computer and Science Lab. My custodian created a Scholar Safety program to keep the campus safe. Our campus security guard became our school's DJ for events. Our cafeteria workers cooked the food from our garden and made snacks for our scholars after school. I can go on and on. So don't forget about the people who are near you. They need to be embraced.

So do our scholars. We all have one scholar who is always in trouble. I had this one scholar named William who was always sent to my office because he was off task or stealing others' things like pencils or erasers. He never thought anything was wrong with it. William would end up in my office four out of five days of the week. I always talked to him about his behavior, but one time I asked him why he did what he did. He told me his teacher did not like him. He said he was "below basic." I asked him how he knew that and he told me because it was on the wall. I decided to do something different and empower him instead. I started calling him "gifted." Whenever I said this to William, his face lit up. I even told his teacher and the entire staff to refer to him as gifted, because, really, all of us are gifted with something. After a few months, William came back to me with a surprise and told me he had moved from below basic and was now basic! He was so proud of himself. I realized at that moment how important it is to empower our youth. I wish I could tell you that all of his behavior issues disappeared. But what I can say is that he believed that he was gifted and therefore it showed in his academic abilities. When we empower our youth, we empower the future.

> **66** *When we talk about our 'community,' we often think within a five-mile radius or so—it's actually much bigger than that.* **99**

Embracing Your External School Community

Your external school community consists of business owners, faith-based organizations, corporations, neighbors, and anyone outside of your school building. If we are going to engage in community partnerships, then it is our job to empower our entire community and more.

Common Threads became one of my strongest partners! I was working in Compton when I met James from Common Threads. I had no idea about this organization and how eager they were to support under-resourced school communities. Common Threads is a national nonprofit that provides children and families cooking and nutrition education to encourage healthy habits that contribute to wellness. They equip under-resourced communities with information to make affordable, nutritious, and appealing food choices wherever they live, work, learn, and play. With James' help, we were able to bring healthy cooking to dozens of schools where there was a lack of healthy food options for kids.

Common Threads brought the partnership of cooking healthy meals to many schools in Compton and Inglewood. It opened up opportunities for them into the culinary world.

When we talk about our "community," we often think within a five-mile radius or so—it's actually much bigger than that. Are you ready for this? Your community is the entire world! Why not? Thanks to technology, we have the ability to reach anyone we want to—anywhere on the globe! When I was a principal and began reaching out to my community through social media, I found out there were many individuals, philanthropists, corporations, and even faith-based organizations who were just as excited as I was about creating access and opportunities for youth.

They had all kinds of ideas that I had not even thought of. Unbeknownst to me, they were willing to go to great lengths to provide all kinds of things like donations of books, school supplies, money, and so much more. When I began reaching out in our neighborhood and beyond, and embracing them, they embraced us right back. Like anything else, it wasn't always easy; it took daily effort. I had to think about my message and anticipate their questions. One time, I wanted to bring a music program to my school. I went to the House of Blues for an event I was invited to. After seeing and hearing the singing, I knew this was what I wanted for my scholars.

I went up to a lady named Victoria Lanier, who was the director of this program called Education Through Music-Los Angeles (ETM-LA).

Victoria Lanier, Executive Director of Education Through Music-Los Angeles

When we met, I explained my reasons for wanting music as an enrichment program for my scholars. She let me know that my school might not be a great fit. I asked her why and she quickly educated me. Schools interested in a partnership should be able to demonstrate that the school leadership, staff, and parents are committed to a school-wide music program and show school-community commitment.

She also went on to share some research and statistics for me on the impact of arts as part of the core curriculum in education and how committed school communities sustain partnerships like this. Kids who play musical instruments are likely to have higher self-esteem, confidence, discipline, concentration, and emotional intelligence than kids who don't play instruments (Hallam, 2010). Kids who are involved with the arts have higher grades and are less likely to drop out of school (Ruppert, 2009). Music education in childhood has been linked to boosts of seven points on IQ scores during childhood (Schellenberg, 2004), and this effect has shown to last beyond high school graduation (Schellenberg, 2006). Children's music education has even been linked to better reading, writing, and mathematical skills (Hallam, 2010).

I understood there was much more to the arts than just an enrichment option for my youth in an afterschool program. Once I embraced the idea, I had to empower my team to embrace it as well. I wish I could tell you it was a smooth process, but it wasn't. While some embraced it immediately, others found it a challenge. This will happen to you on your community empowerment journey.

A lot of communication helped. Victoria was willing to meet with my team and share information about the role of arts in education as she did with me. Her team provided several professional development workshops and listened to our challenges as well. This helped tremendously. We decided to accept the challenge, even though we were still met with doubts and resistance from some. I am glad we did because the arts ultimately became monumentally embraced at our school. In fact, when I tried to make any adjustments from year to year, no one wanted me to do so. The arts and music had become something we embraced and became part of our school culture. Remember, community empowerment is a process.

A Lesson About Empowerment

If we are really going to empower our communities, then we need to move from the idea of engagement to empowerment (Eury, 2018). That may sound like a simple concept, but it is not an easy thing to do. As I have visited many school campuses, I have seen various strategies people use to engage their communities. I have seen carnivals, think tanks, clubs, town-hall meetings, steering committees, dances, auctions, car washes, fundraisers, pep rallies, career days, poetry nights, literacy and math nights, concerts, and the list goes on and on.

While many of these were done with good intentions, I often wondered if the people involved were truly empowered or just engaged for the day or the moment. It's a question that deserves thought because if they were just engaged, they participated and left. This happened in all of the schools in which I served as principal until I really understood the concept of empowerment.

Community empowerment goes beyond buy-in and leans into ownership (Ripp, 2014). When community partners feel like they are a part of something, they feel vested. How can we make this happen as educators? Over the years, I have been fortunate enough to have garnered over 200 community partners. They have helped us do things we could not do without them. Each one taught me something as a leader that helped me become a more effective one.

Not long ago, I learned about one organization out of Canada that taught me about empowerment: WE Charity. WE Charity came into my life when I attended an exciting event called WE Day. I went to see what the buzz was all about, as I heard about it from other community partners. As I walked around aimlessly, watching the star-studded live performances and hearing the screams from the thousands of scholars leaping up and down, I was rescued by a WE Day worker who asked me if I was lost. I guess it showed on my face.

66 When community partners feel like they are a part of something, they feel vested. How can we make this happen as educators? 99

I told her it was my first time. She led me to the back and shared with me the mission of WE schools. She explained how they were teaching youth to be change agents and problem-solvers and to be concerned about their communities and the world.

The following year, I was able to bring my entire district to WE Day. There was no cost to get in. They earned their tickets by collaboratively working on a WE Day project that could help the community. Some schools made care packets for the homeless, collected clothes for those in shelters, or held a recycling program.

We were surrounded by hundreds of kids who were jumping up and down at the live performance of Alicia Keys. And then one of the strangest things happened. One of the excited high school scholars (whom I did not know) turned around and shouted, "You are going to be up there next year!" Julie and I looked at each other with confused looks on our faces. Then as we were leaving, an usher at the Forum hugged me and told me the same. Little did I know, they were right.

It was inspiring to watch so many young people who were empowered and ready to take on the world. After many years in the K–12 public school sector, I had thought I had seen it all. This was very different from what I was used to. This was like school unleashed! They were not just having fun dancing and singing—they were learning! I saw it in their faces. There was a sense of empowerment I had not seen before. They were well-behaved and the celebrities helped to make it an exciting event. But more than the fanfare, stars, and music, it was the message of service learning. I know that was another new "Why Not?" moment for me.

What can I say about the founders of WE? Craig and Marc Kielburger are humanitarians, activists, and social entrepreneurs! Over 20 years ago, they set out on a bold mission: to work with developing communities to free children and their families from poverty and exploitation. Their vision expanded to include empowering youth at home, connecting them with global issues and social causes, and partnering with schools to inspire young change-makers from within the classroom.

Craig believes that service learning is about building connections between the classroom and the community that deepen student learning and make a meaningful, measurable social impact on the world. In my district, we were able to implement WE in every school.

Craig and Marc Kielburger taught me what empowerment really means for scholars when I traveled with them on an educational leaders trip to the Maasai Mara in Kenya. It forever changed my perspective of teaching and learning.

WE Schools' service-learning program is multilayered and works through four steps. First, scholars investigate an issue they care about, learning about its root causes and how they can make an impact. Then, they use what they've learned to develop an action plan, focusing on how they can rally their peers and community to make the greatest possible impact. They execute their plan, and finally, they take time to measure their impact and reflect on the skills they developed, such as information literacy, critical thinking, leadership, and empathy.

Imagine a student who cares about local hunger designing the budget for a soup kitchen as part of her math lesson, or scholars in an art class honing their skills by designing posters for a fundraiser to build a school in a developing community. In these courses, scholars don't just learn the hard skills needed to excel at curriculum objectives—they see why those skills matter for making an impact!

That is what I wanted! We were able to partner with WE Charity and help bring the message of service learning to every school in the Inglewood Unified School District. You know, if it were not for meeting WE, my understanding of empowerment would be diminished today. While I learned about the importance of community empowerment, WE taught me about global empowerment. As educators, we may not have all the answers, which is why we need community partners to help us broaden our insight, knowledge, and understanding. I think it is so important to seek out other partners who share your interest but can also teach you different ways of getting there. There is a motto that WE uses that helps me remember why empowerment is so important: WE makes doing good, doable. I agree wholeheartedly!

Action Steps for Embracing Your Community

1 Go Door Knocking

I can truly say this was one of the most important things I ever did as a principal when I needed to empower my community. Think about it this way: Your school is the hub of growth, development, and the future of the community. They need to know you and you need to know them.

I did community door knocking once a month, religiously. I enrolled different individuals from my staff or parent volunteers to walk with me. We put on our tennis shoes and went from one business door to the next. The businesses loved it! They even looked forward to seeing us on the streets every month. They got to know me by name and I knew theirs. I remember one store owner yelling out, "Hi, Dr. Sanderlin!"

Action Steps

and I yelled back, "Hi, Charlie." We tried to visit new businesses each month to widen our outreach.

Some business owners and employees gave us water bottles when we came by. A woman from the church on the corner thanked us for coming by and the pastor from the local church became a volunteer. One family even made us breakfast sandwiches for our journey back to the school. We saw the community become empowered because we took time to embrace them.

If and when you go door knocking, there are some things to keep in mind so you will be successful. Focus on the people you meet and not so much on your school and what it offers. When your community realizes you came out to get to know them, they will be more open to share. Generally, people like to talk about themselves and their business or passion projects, so be ready to listen. Focus on learning as much as you can and showing appreciation for their time.

Also, while you will have a basic message in your mind, try and be authentic. Allow each conversation to flow in the direction it goes. Smile and be generous with your time. Remember why you are doing this: You are embracing your community.

Walking door to door with community leader and former Inglewood Rotary President, Dexter Hall. This was a game changer for me that made embracing communities real.

2 Let Your School Community Get to Know You

While it's crucial for you to get to know your community, it is equally important for your community to get to know you. I don't mean the "educator" you. I mean the real you. You see, this is how genuine relationships are born. This goes beyond the smile and wave of the hand as you drive by and head home. You can do this with small conversations, newsletters, social media, or community meetings. It is important to have many ways to introduce yourself to your community. The important thing is that you do it and become intentional about it.

3 Show Hospitality

Inviting the community in is a sure way to embrace them.
There is nothing like a great host. If you know me, I love to entertain and host parties at my home. I especially enjoy welcoming people who are coming for the first time. I do a lot of preparation to make sure things are just right and I want to make them feel comfortable while they are there. I want everyone who comes to remember the hospitality they were shown. Trust me, people remember my parties for a long time and call me each year to see when I am hosting another one. I am inviting a community of people (those I know and don't know) to my home. I have some friends who wonder why I don't use a hall or a private dining room at a restaurant. I tell them because I want to bring them to my home and for me there is no greater way to show hospitality.

I feel like the same is true when we host community events. Your school is your "home" in a way. A long time ago, they used to call it the "schoolhouse." As you begin empowering your community, think about how you can use your schoolhouse to embrace your community and show them hospitality. When you do, this means going beyond passing out agendas, name tags, and a sign-in form. Hospitality means community embracement.

4 Provide Food

You would think this would go without saying, but I am still seeing the absence of food at community events. Folks, water is good, but not enough! I am sorry, I don't think donuts are enough either if you do it all the time. If you can provide a meal every once in a while, they will never forget you. In fact, this is a great opportunity to ask a restaurant owner or the general manager to provide food for your events. Let them know that you want to provide a delicious lunch for a school community event. Why not? It is a win-win for them, too! I did this all the time. In fact, McDonald's, Costco, Panera Bread, Sam's Club, Subway, and SchoolsFirst Federal Credit Unions would often provide food for our community events for free! I met with several of their Directors of Community Affairs, who were looking for opportunities to support positive community events like ours. They did it time after time, and we also recognized them as partners in education on our main office wall.

5 Going Beyond the Meeting

Having another "meeting" has a way of turning away a community. If you are tired of trying to get the community to come to another meeting, stop having them. I am talking about embracing your community and building bridges. Sometimes, "meetings" have a negative connotation. I would suggest calling them gatherings, think tanks, or thought circles. Your community will be more willing to come to something that sounds positive, empowering, and inviting, rather than a meeting, which feels like rules and boredom.

6 Listen

I remember the late Dr. Genevieve Shepherd, the longtime principal of Tom Bradley Environmental Science and Humanities Charter Magnet School in the Los Angeles Unified School District. She was the queen of community empowerment in my book! She taught me to deeply care and listen to the heartbeat of the community. Not just say it, but mean it. She would embrace her (internal and external) community every day. When I was a young, green principal, Dr. Shepherd would allow me and other new principals to learn from her. I would simply grab a chair and sit in the corner of her office and watch her work for hours.

I was amazed at the many people whom she spoke with and reached out to. She embraced everyone! She met with business owners, CEOs, philanthropists, potential partners, teachers, staff, and yes, even local vagrants who roamed the community. They respected her and never posed a threat to her school or her scholars.

In addition to the many adults she spent time with, Dr. Shepherd ALWAYS took time to listen to her scholars. No topic was too trivial. Sometimes, I would overhear her trying to get them to understand why it was wrong to jump in line before the other person or why borrowing a pencil from someone else and not giving it back was stealing. She was always ready to embrace them.

Dr. Shepherd was a very well-dressed woman who always wore matching colors and big, flamboyant hats. She was a true sight for sore eyes. I wanted to be just like her. Every time I left her school, I either felt affirmed or ready to do better. I learned most of what I know about embracing the community directly from the queen. She would tell me, "Dr. Sanderlin, your job is to serve your community. Don't forget that." That stuck with me and also haunted me whenever I forgot it.

 FURTHERING THE CONVERSATION

Empowered Schools, Empowered Students: Creating Connected and Invested Learners
by Pernille S. Ripp

This book helps you empower teachers and students to regain control of their own teaching and learning journey. With this helpful guide, cultivate enthusiasm for learning by changing the power dynamic and putting the reins back into the hands of students. Administrators and teachers learn to:

- Cultivate the experts at their school.
- Create an environment of trust and collaboration.
- Give students and staff a voice.

The book includes real-life stories from other connected educators! Transform the learning experience and create lasting change with this breakthrough volume.

Take the Why Not? Challenge: Go Door Knocking!

Invite a few of your school volunteers to accompany you as you go door knocking to every business around your school community. Get out of your comfort zone and just go! Try a new block each time. You will become more confident and the buzz will get around. Trust me, when you take time to embrace your internal and external community, you will come to be more empowered and your entire community will, too.

Below are some easy tips that helped me:

- Block out sufficient time on your calendar. I suggest at least an hour at a time.
- Get some others to walk with you—don't go alone.
- Wear comfortable shoes.
- Smile and be authentic.
- Introduce yourself and say hello.
- Actively listen and lean in.
- Don't go empty-handed. Bring your cards or school brochures so that the people in the community can learn about your mission, vision, goals, and programs.

 REFLECTION PROMPTS

- **What skills do you need to work on to be able to embrace your community more effectively?**
- **How can your school be more inviting to the community?**
- **What inhibitions do you have when you think about embracing your community?**
- **Is there someone you can learn from to help you embrace your community better?**

Unleash Your Passion and Pursue Relationships

I f you are anything like me, you believe, without a shadow of a doubt, you are divinely called to the field of education. It is who you are—not simply what you do. You know what I am talking about? When you should be sleeping, you are up thinking about ways to make life better for your school. When you should be having family time, you find yourself stealing away to plan for

the next day. My son always seems to find me when I am in the middle of a school project I am working on. It is an ongoing challenge for me to balance the two parts of my life. For me, it's just because I am super passionate about what I do.

Educators will never be paid what we ought to be and there are many complexities that go along with our profession. Yet, we keep coming back. I call that passion. In this chapter, I want to talk about passion and how we should use that to pursue relationships. Empowering our communities is a verb. It is an action. We actually have to do something to make that happen.

> **"** *I would venture to say that your passion for your school is really at the heart of where all community empowerment is birthed.* **"**

Passion is powerful! It has the unique ability to touch other people. For me, that is the beginning of a relationship. Passion is also contagious. I would venture to say that your passion for your school is really at the heart of where all community empowerment is birthed.

Sometimes you can learn more about passion and relationships when you travel. Last summer, I was invited by the WE Charity to attend the Senior Educators Professional Learning Trip to the Maasai Mara region of Kenya, Africa. As I discussed in the previous chapter, the WE organization is an international development charity and youth empowerment movement founded by Marc and Craig Kielburger. They were only kids when they founded it, but they were kids on a mission to empower other kids. They continue focusing on service learning where the scholars take the lead and full ownership of their own learning. It was an honor to travel with them abroad to observe and learn from other educators.

While in Kenya, each day consisted of a significant amount of professional learning to enhance deeper understanding of global competencies and international development. We interacted with the Kenyan community, volunteered in safety training, took part in Swahili language lessons, learned how to collect water from the local mamas, learned traditional methods of Maasai beading, trained in the art of Maasai weaponry, and embarked on a safari in the Maasai Mara.

We also visited educators (facilitators) and scholars (learners) at local WE schools. The learners took us on a tour and they each spoke about the school mission, vision, and goals. The facilitators stood in the background. It was amazing to watch! My heart warmed up as I listened to them passionately speak about their school. One of the learners told me that they were encouraged to help make the daily schedule and design the new school facility that was currently being built. They were clearly empowered in a way I had not seen before. I knew that when I returned to the United States, community empowerment would be a priority for me.

My school's partnership with the iMusic United Foundation changed my thinking about how partnerships are truly relationships. This program brought music to my school for students who never experienced it before. When I met the founder, Miho Nomura, I did not know we would become friends. She is one of the most powerful women in the music industry and finds time to personally come to each school and make sure they are getting a quality program. But that is what a partnership should be. It can evolve and grow. Because of our relationship, we impacted thousands of students in underserved communities. So build relationships with your partners so you can multiply your impact!

66 If you don't share your passion for your school, who will know about it? If they don't know, how can they work with you or help you? 99

I realize that communicating your passion may not come naturally to all educators and it may feel somewhat uncomfortable. I also felt that way in the beginning, but I got better over time. Think of it like this: If you don't share your passion for your school, who will know about it? If they don't know, how can they work with you or help you? Those questions helped me to overcome some of my natural fears. Whenever I led with my passion, it was easier to pursue new relationships.

Remember, we all express our passion differently. Maybe you tend to be a quiet person or more reserved. That is okay. There are a million different ways that you can share your passion.

Pursuing Relationships

Let's talk about pursuing relationships. If your only goal is to land a partnership, you may fall flat on your face. What I know for sure about partners is that they can smell a fake a mile away. Your ability to empower your community and be transparent will be your success. I remember a partnership my school had with a local business called Pizza Studio. The manager, Art, was looking for a school to partner with, and what he did was admirable. This manager took time to visit every school in our district. He could have just dropped off his flyers or his card, but he didn't. When he visited my school, he made it abundantly clear he wanted to establish relationships with the schools he was hoping to partner with. He wanted to develop a relationship with the principal, get to know the staff, and see if there was a possibility for a partnership.

Community partnerships are a win-win situation for the school and the business!

That is exactly what happened! The moment we met was magical. We both could not stop talking about the different ways we might partner. I think this is where I learned that pursuing relationships can turn into partnerships. He wanted to provide opportunities for schools within his community to do fundraising. Schools would be able to have a pizza night, invite parents and others to come, and keep 50% of the profits raised. Not only that, each school took part in a contest to see who raised the most. People and families came from all over to help support their school of choice. It was a win-win situation because Pizza Studio became even more popular and made more sales. The healthy competition was great for everyone involved. Everyone wanted to win! This was a great way to empower each school's community.

Because of our relationship, we were able to multiply the partnership with every school in the district. We also included other businesses, such as Red Lobster, Friday's, Home Depot, and others within our local shopping center. Whatever you do, seek a relationship first! There are countless surprises that will develop from the relationships you make, like a strong partnership or even a friendship.

Needless to say, Art and I are still friends and often reflect on how many schools were positively impacted. We love to share our story with other school leaders who want a partnership before a relationship. Think about what relationships you need to foster within your community. When you meet people, business leaders, politicians, or even celebrities, relationships are waiting for you and the rest will simply come.

Walgreen's became a partner with WE Charity to support teachers across North America. This partnership was available to educators nationwide at no cost, equipping them with the tools and resources to address critical social issues in their classrooms. I had the opportunity to help them build relationships with schools all across North America providing free tools and resources, professional development, and curriculum. This is more than a partnership—this is a relationship.

I was proud to be an Ambassador for the Walgreen's WE Teachers Award that supplied teachers around the country with school supples.

Action Steps for Unleashing Your Passion and Pursuing Relationships

1 Make New Friends

Take time to get to know the community around your school and beyond. I like to think of it as making new friends. If you do, you will approach it differently and less robotically. It is not a contest. It is an effort to get to know your community better. These actions will serve you well as you empower your community.

Are there corporations, mom-and-pop stores, or a mixture of both? Are there mostly single-family homes or apartments? Are there older or younger families? This is your opportunity to introduce yourself and make new friends. You can certainly use the Internet to research your community, but I highly recommend taking a drive or a walk around the community for a personal approach. Observe the people, culture, and the climate and you will be amazed at what you will see and learn. By doing this, you will grow in the eyes of the community because you found it necessary to come out of your office and meet them.

2 Smile

I have to admit, I have gotten more free meals with a smile than anything else! A smile has the power to break all kinds of boundaries and build all kinds of connections. It can light up a room and cause people to ask you, "Where you are from?" Many people think I am from the South because I tend to smile a lot. In truth, I am a California girl. But when I do smile, it seems to be a magnet. It has really helped me start many new relationships.

All of us have experienced this at a restaurant, movie theatre, or any place of business. When the clerk fails to smile, people notice it. The lack of a smile is usually translated as bad customer service. However, when they do smile, the aura in the room is changed and often produces a smile on your own face. A relationship has begun without a word ever spoken. That is the power of a smile.

If smiling does not come naturally for you, I get it. Practice it in the mirror. Sometimes you have to fake it until you make it, my friend. At some point, it will become automatic and your community will be drawn to it. A smile directed at someone is like a welcome mat in front of a doorway. So break out that piano smile and make some music! New community relationships are awaiting you. When you visit businesses, talk to people, or see them on the street, smile. They will ask you questions, which will be a great opportunity for you to talk about your school and learn about them. Before you know it, a new relationship has begun and cards have been exchanged.

3 Find Your Theme Song

When I was a principal making daily outreach efforts in my community, I rarely did so without listening to my theme song, "Ain't No Stoppin Us Now" by McFadden and Whitehead. I love this song because every now and then, I have to remind myself that nothing will stop me, regardless of how hard it gets. It keeps me going and often gives me confidence to reach out to businesses in my school community and beyond. I play it everywhere—in my car, on my phone, and in my head. It pumps me up and the lyrics remind me why I need to unleash my passion and pursue relationships.

Whatever your song is, play it everywhere you go so you can inspire yourself! Your theme song serves to encourage and empower you. Write down the lyrics that speak to you on a sticky note and post it around your house and in your car. This will serve as a reminder and motivate you. I love finding out what other people's theme songs are. My husband's theme song is "Ain't No Mountain High Enough" and our son's is "My Way" by Frank Sinatra. I love my dad's theme song, which is "Get On Up" by James Brown. What's yours?

Friends, you will need a theme song because pursuing relationships is not always easy. It takes a lot of hard work, planning, confidence, time, and courage. You will also get rejections along the way. This can be discouraging at times. But if you have a little song to sing or a hymn to hum, the load gets a little bit lighter and you get back out there. We all need something from the outside, working on the inside to empower us to face the community head on!

4 Talk, Talk, and Talk Some More

While listening to your community is important, also be ready to talk about your school to people you meet in the community.
A quiet mouth will never get fed, so speak up! What do you talk about? Be ready to talk about your school's mission, vision, and goals to anyone who will listen. Choose to be passionate about your school, even if you don't feel like it. I admit, there are some days when this is hard to do. Sometimes I feel like I had all of the passion sucked out of me by daily problems, disappointments, and the lack of funding or resources. But let's face it: No one wants to hear the sad stories about our schools anymore. They don't want to hear them because they already know them. Maybe not all the gritty details, but they've heard about the kinds of struggles we face.

Speaking at a community meeting hosted by the Goodwill Southern California Store. You can find opportunities to meet new partners everywhere.

Focus on what is working and what you are hopeful for, regardless of the obstacles in your path. That kind of talk gives people goosebumps. And folks, goosebumps can turn into a relationship and eventually into a partnership. When you talk, they will listen, especially if you are talking about possibilities for your school. In my experience, whenever I began talking about our school's hopes, dreams, and possibilities, people in the community saw themselves in it. They began to engage in dreaming and planning. This kind of conversation can lead to many things. Choose to talk about the positive and the opportunities for community support.

FURTHERING THE CONVERSATION

Powerful Partnerships: A Teacher's Guide to Engaging Families for Success

by Karen Mapp, Ilene Carver, and Jessica Lander

In a message that provokes and inspires, and in language that is clear and discerning, *Powerful Partnerships* is at once a practical and informative guide for teachers, a revelatory and poignant narrative of family-school engagement, and a bold and urgent call to action. The authors are wise and empathic guides, challenging teachers to interrogate their own core values, urging them to develop an ethical stance and cultural competency that will support student learning, and offering them a path forward across the terrain of parent-teacher relationships.

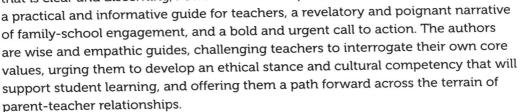

Take the Why Not? Challenge: Meet Five People!

Your passion wants to get out anyway, so will you please let it out? I want you to go out in your community today and meet five people you don't know! These people may be business leaders, politicians, or simply people in the supermarket buying groceries. Listen, new relationships can be made everywhere. They are not always in the places you think. I have some quick tips for you below that may make it easier.

1. Smile graciously at EVERYONE YOU SEE. In fact, be intentional about this. Smile first—don't wait for them.

2. If a conversation strikes up, find a way to share your school story. Talk about how great it is and the opportunities it offers. Talk about your dreams and why it's the best school you know. People will see the gleam in your eye and feel your passion.

3. Let them know you are always looking for community support and engagement to create access and opportunities for your youth.

4. Listen to people's stories and show genuine interest. They may begin sharing how they can help.

5. Invite them to be a guest reader or schedule a lunch with them to continue the conversation.

6. Don't leave without sharing contact information. Always keep business cards with you. That is the link so you can follow up with them.

Unleash your passion on everyone you meet, wherever you are, and see what happens! Your passion will be the engine in your community empowerment machine! Have fun!

 REFLECTION PROMPTS

- **What are you passionate about?**

- **What makes you smile when you think about your school?**

- **Whom can you start a conversation with today in your community?**

- **What is your theme song?**

Why Not? Challenge #4
Find Your School's Hook

When I think of a school hook, I think about that one thing that hooks me as I read about the school. It could be a specific theme like STEM, STEAM, Arts, Medicine, Entrepreneurship, Innovation, etc.

You might be thinking about your vision or your mission. You should! Your school hook or theme should be in direct alignment to your mission and your vision. None of these should be different or separate. I can remember when we made our school's hook the arts. It became part of everything we wrote, did, and said.

A school's "hook" can be the central source of community empowerment. It's your school's brand that can be the key ingredient that your community can repeat. Larry Cuban (1998) argues that good schools come in many styles. What is your school style? You might not think of it like that. Heck, I meet many educators who don't even see their school as a business, but it is.

We are in the business of educating children and young adults. Every business has a market, content, and a message. Why should a school be any different just because it houses youth? Today, our communities are becoming more and more aware of that fact. They drive past schools and no longer have to wonder what is going on behind the four walls. Schools are starting to use banners, digital marquees, murals, social media, and more to get the word out! They want the community to know who they are and the programs they offer. This is called branding. In fact, you can walk into the main office at most schools and see a monitor there rolling various pictures and videos about their school happenings. That can be a school hook.

> 66 *Your school hook or theme should be in direct alignment to your mission and your vision. None of these should be different or separate.* 99

Your hook brings character to your school. School character is closely linked to school effectiveness! (Hill, Foster, and Gendler, 1990) Many times a school hook is in the name. Is your school named after a dead president? That is the case of many of our public schools. While it is wonderful to name a school after someone who has impacted the world, I find that when I visit these schools, there is little knowledge about the name or the person behind the name. Now it is popular to name schools after ideals or acronyms that mean something.

The point I am trying to make is that communities have always been empowered by school names and mascots. They represent history and good old times. If you want to empower and increase community support, think about changing the name, creating a new focus of the name, or adding to the name.

Of course, none of this can be done by yourself. It takes almost an act of Congress to change a school name. Fortunately, it will take an act of community empowerment.

When I worked at Foster Elementary, my school staff and I wanted to be a school of the arts, however, we had no art anywhere in the school, let alone any paintbrushes or other materials. So we decided to paint our theme on the wall facing the community and it read, "Fostering Learning Through the Arts!" This was a game changer for us. And that small name change made such a difference with future partners who wanted to bring even more arts opportunities to our scholars. Soon we partnered with City Hearts, who brought theatre, dance, and photography classes to our school. Many times one partner can make way for lots of other related partnerships.

Just the addition to our Foster name became more noticeable to the community. It became our hook! Our attendance grew and we suddenly had purpose. Now parents and community members knew what was going on behind the four walls. They became so interested, many of them wanted to help out. Soon we began receiving all kinds of donations, such as paintbrushes, musical instruments, and much more! What is your school hook? Below are some action steps to help you find, reestablish, or sharpen your hook.

Action Steps for Finding Your School's Hook

1 Have a School Story Summit

Holding a School Story Summit would be a great opportunity to invite your community business leaders to your school.
The purpose of the summit is to gain a clear narrative about your school and its purpose. Now, we all know your primary purpose is to educate, but it is much more than that.

Having a clear narrative about your school is the strongest hook one can have. Get a team together and draft your ideas on chart paper. Make it authentic and aligned to your school's core beliefs. By inviting people from the community, you will be surprised at the information that will come out that no one knew, not even you. It will be a great time of learning and rejoicing about where the school is going and the rich history it came from. School stories build school pride!

Your school story also develops a common language for people in the community. You want everyone saying the same thing. It is like singing the same song and it gets louder and louder. After a while, no one needs to read the words because they memorized it. That is what you want with your school story—the entire community will be able to articulate the hook. That creates empowerment. Whenever anyone in an organization becomes knowledgeable of the mission, vision, goals, updates, highlights,

and stories, they feel empowered! They feel a part of it because they are informed. There is no difference with schools. Every school has a story and it's up to you to share it. If you don't, who will?

2 Enroll Everyone

As I said, this is a collaborative process where you will want to engage your community. Consider inviting local community business leaders into this process. When you encourage your community to give input, you will get new ideas and unsuspected community support. This is shared leadership when you bring your community to the table to have open dialogue.

You should reach out and invite your local businesses, store owners, employees, CEOs, managers, supervisors, church leaders, community groups, politicians—the list goes on. Their voices are important and valued. When you enroll others, you go beyond just inviting them to get an agenda and sign in. That is true ownership!

3 Make Your Brand Visible

Basically, your hook is your brand! Makes sense, right? What good is it to have a school hook unless other people know about it? Shout it from the mountaintop! You want people to drive past your school and say, "Wow, look at what they are doing!" Once you have a brand, market it! Use banners, a marquee, social media, T-shirts, or any of your real estate to get the word out! In this era of information, there is no shortage of ways to communicate.

The visibility of a school hook is another way to speak to the community without having meetings, gatherings, or events. You may already have a marquee, but you are not using it. You may have social media, but no one is posting on a regular basis. Maybe you have great events, but no one is taking pictures or interviewing the community to get feedback. All of these examples help to push your brand so the community can help carry the message.

Action Steps

Think about your school walls. Can you use them for murals to showcase positive programs you have? Think about your front office when the community walks in. What do they see? What do you want them to know? Think about your newsletters. Do they display your mission, vision, goals, or school hook? Your school is a canvas waiting for a masterpiece. Who will be the artist?

4 Research Other School Hooks

It is always good to know what other schools are doing outside of your district. Go online and see what other schools are saying. Look at public, private, and charter schools in your area and in different states. Check out everyone and see what they are conveying about their schools. By doing so, it may give you an idea of what you need to say about yours.

Find out how other schools have enrolled their community. You can learn new strategies this way. Interview principals from these schools. Education is a lifelong process and we learn from each other.

I would often call other school principals and compliment them on their work. I would ask them how they empowered their community to action and how they helped to move their school hook, mission, vision, and goals. This is another way you can build new relationships with other colleagues and learn what they do. None of us have all the answers and getting out to see other schools can be very refreshing. We can always learn from others and replicate what they are doing. When you take from one person, it is stealing. When you take from many, it is called research. At least, that is how I look at it.

5 Attend Community Events/Functions

Not only is it important for you to enroll the community, it is equally essential to find out where the community watering holes are. Going to mixers and rubbing shoulders with people will open up opportunities for you to share your school's hook!

I went to places like the Rotary Club meetings, Chamber of Commerce meetings, Elks Lodge meetings, City Council meetings, and even the city pastoral meetings for faith-based organizations. I even became a member of the quarterly community meetings for PBS television programming because they wanted to get feedback on their content. I went and there were many opportunities for me to meet people, talk about my school, and build relationships. You never know who is listening or whom you may be talking to. When you are open to attending meetings, you will learn of community gatherings you never heard of.

Let me tell you now, get your clothes ready and cards in hand. Don't forget, you are the representative of your school and you are introducing it to the community. At these functions, you can easily ignite a spark of community empowerment around your school! But if you are not there, it could be a missed opportunity. I usually find out about these events on social media or by word of mouth in the community.

When I talked about making your brand visible, I also mean YOU! You are the best brand spokesperson for your school. But this will have minimal impact unless you get out into the community. By doing so, you will create interest, intrigue, and "community" around your school hook. People will get excited just as much as you are. Attending community events and functions is also a great way to build relationships.

 FURTHERING THE CONVERSATION

How to Help Your School Thrive Without Breaking the Bank
by John G. Gabriel and Paul C. Farmer

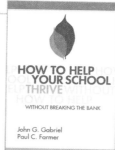

Yes, times are tough and money is tight, but the good news is that you already have the resources you need to help your school thrive. Here's a book that will help you maximize them. Two experienced educators explain how to improve your school with internally developed, inexpensive, and time-efficient programs and initiatives, including:

- Assembling shared leadership and mission oversight teams.
- Using a SMART framework to organize your school's goals.
- Developing homegrown formative assessments.
- Planning delayed openings and/or early dismissals for staff development.
- Identifying stages of team development that lead to more productive and time-efficient meetings.
- Recruiting data champions among your staff to benchmark your improvement efforts.

Take the Why Not? Challenge: Revisit Your School's Hook

Do you ever wonder what the community thinks as they pass by your school? My grandmother always said, "If you want people to think something about you, tell them." So get with your team and jot down thoughts and ideas. Be willing to scrap your old mission and vision statement if it no longer defines your school. Make a commitment to take time this week to look at your mission and rewrite it, if necessary. Keep it short and simple! Be clear about your school's hook and tell the world! The community is listening.

1. Invite some people from your community to sit on your leadership team to give input to the school hook.

2. Chart everyone's ideas down on chart paper for everyone to see.

3. Once you have decided on a specific hook, make it visible! Add it to your website, make a banner, or paint it on the wall. Think about putting it on T-shirts, too...that is a fun way to get the word out on the street! (Please make sure to follow your school districts' approval process for changing/adding to school names, logos, or websites.)

4. Get ready for community empowerment!

 REFLECTION PROMPTS

- **What is your school's hook?**
- **How can you make your school's hook more visible?**
- **Which community members will you invite to sit on your leadership team?**
- **What community events are you attending?**

Elevate Your School's "Why" (Your Cause)

This chapter is about knowing why your school exists. This is a very different conversation and will be a make-or-break moment when it comes to developing partnerships.

Your community needs to know your school's "why." Why does it exist? You should be able to explain not only what it offers, but why it offers what it does. That is a much deeper conversation and takes some quiet time to discover. Your school's "why" is your cause!

I believe, as leaders, it is probably the most important thing we can come to terms with.

Let me give you an example. A friend of mine was the principal of a dual-immersion school in Inglewood, California. He took time to walk to each home in his school community to discuss why their school was needed. Their school hook was having a dual-immersion program, but he wanted them to know why that was important. He wanted them to know that their school was intentional about making sure every child who walked through their doors would be proficient in both languages. He explained why this would be beneficial for their future.

Your community may find it much easier to connect to your school's "why" than your "what." Your "why" is where the soul of your school lives. It is your cause that keeps you up at night and burdens you during the day because that is why you come to work. It is the "why" that will empower your community to stand with you and work with you. DuFour and Eaker (1998) challenge members of a group to reflect on the fundamental purpose of the organization, and ask, "Why do we exist?", "What are we here to do together?", and "What is the business of our business?"

Talking About My School's Cause

One evening, I was invited to attend an event at a home in prestigious Beverly Hills. I had a chance to speak about my school but they only gave me two minutes. When I was done, I met someone who said something to me that I will never forget. He told me he came to this event specifically to meet me. Tom Shadyac was not only a film director and producer, having directed popular films such as *Ace Ventura: Pet Detective*, *The Nutty Professor*, and *Bruce Almighty*, he also has a heart of gold. Tom had a vision to "pay it forward" and I had a vision to partner with him. Not long after we met, he came to my school and told me to bring my fifth-grade students to the playground because he had something for them. He drove into our school grounds with a truck and emptied out over a hundred brand-new bicycles and safety gear. Tom's

generosity reminded me of this very important lesson:
Never be too quiet about your cause. You never know who is listening.
It could very well be your next partner.

I was blown away to find out that Ellen DeGeneres was interested in our school and how we empowered the community and developed so many community partners. She was a close friend of Tom's, and the rest is history. He was empowered and she became empowered. Empowerment can travel! The next thing I knew, Ellen brought her entire crew and filmed us live for her show from our school cafeteria. I had no idea that she was going to give us a $50,000 check. That was a moment in my career that I will say catapulted my efforts in the community partnership world. I received calls and emails from all over the world after that.

66 Your school's "why" is your cause! I believe, as leaders, it is probably the most important thing we can come to terms with. 99

Sometimes articulating your school's cause motivates your entire community. At one point my school library was small, dark, dingy, and quite frankly, was never going to motivate anyone to read. I had a big vision of how this library should look but a very small budget. I remember visiting other school and public libraries and being amazed at how beautiful they were. Why couldn't our library be like that? One day, I decided to go to a farmer's market where there were a lot of people on a Saturday afternoon. I took a chair, sat down, and made a sign that read: "Please give books to our school." Several hours went by and people came by and dropped off books by my side.

I was excited at all the books we were getting when a woman drove by, rolled down her window, and told me I could get up from my seat now. She introduced me to an organization called Access Books. I never heard of Access Books (www.accessbooks.net) before, but they brought me hundreds of books and a beautiful couch for our new library.

The idea of building a new library from scratch began to empower the entire community! A gentleman came and built all the shelves, while others came and helped paint murals. I saw teachers, scholars, board members, local politicians, parents, and business owners all coming to help get our new library in order. It was the greatest motivator for literacy that we could have imagined, and I know it could not have been done without the community pitching in their support.

In my experience, every successful community partnership is built around a cause. In fact, the work of community empowerment and partnerships is almost entirely cause-driven.

Last year, I visited Freeport Intermediate School in Freeport, Texas. I was welcomed by a huge banner that read, "Whatever It Takes!" Before speaking to anyone, I understood this school's "why." As I walked the campus, I saw the same message throughout the hallways, offices, and classrooms.

I was welcomed by this banner at Freeport Intermediate School in Freeport, Texas. Once I entered, I knew their "why."

By the end of my visit, I realized these words served a greater purpose than to just be pretty banners or cute decorations. Their "why" (cause) was elevated by everyone. The entire community knew every child who walked into their building will learn, no matter what it takes.

Action Steps for Elevating Your "Why"

1 Turn Down the Volume

Knowing your "why" will come from deep inside. It is worth getting quiet and reflecting on this. Take your time to think more about why your school exists and how it may add value to the community. I always believed that when any business takes up real estate, it owes it to the community to share why it does. Why does your school exist?

2 Turn Up the Volume

If the only person who knows your "why" is you, then you need to get louder. Price (2008) asserts that another important audience is the collection of community groups that need to be mobilized. Sometimes we are so passionate as school leaders that we forget to engage others in our "why."

When you turn up the volume, you tell the community about your school using every communication channel available! You continuously find opportunities to speak, share, or "have words." You put ads on social media, create T-shirts and paraphernalia, you go live on social media, and you become the poster child for your school. Who is a better advocate? It should be you! Not your test scores or the medals you've won. It should be you and your community. After a while, your community will be doing all the talking!

3 Get Excited About Your Cause

When you are excited about your cause, others will be as well. If you are not excited about your school community, don't expect others to be. As a school/district leader, your excitement and passion can lead the way. Make your school cause your purpose and driving force to come to work every day. Noel Tichy (1997) contends that great leaders are able to translate the purpose and priorities of their organizations into a few big ideas that unite people and give them a sense of direction in their day-to-day work. Your school's "why" can be that sense of direction and your moral compass.

Communities form around common characteristics, experiences, practices, or beliefs that are important enough to bind members to one another in a kind of fellowship (Carey & Frohnen, 1998). That is the kind of excitement you want to stir up in your community if you have not done so already. That excitement will come from your school's "why."

4 Do Something Drastic

One year, our main school cause was to increase literacy school-wide. Our reading scores were dismal and something had to be done. Our existing library was old, dark, and dingy. How could we embrace literacy and our library be so outdated? I just believed a new library would increase the joy of reading. So I had to do something drastic.

I went to an open-air farmer's market. I took a chair, sat down, and wrote our literacy cause on a poster. It read, "Please Give Books to Our School." While I was mildly successful with a few people, it came to me that I was more focused on our "what" than our "why." It was not about just getting books. It was really about developing readers. Do you see the difference?

So I took my marker and changed it to "Please partner with our school so our scholars can become great readers." That was it! That was our school's "why": our cause! Our intention was to increase literacy. That is a world of difference from just getting books!

Our cause resonated with people so much that I was there until late in the evening surrounded by hundreds of books. Others came by and talked to me about the importance of reading and how a book had changed their lives. Before I knew it, various people who were once shopping for lettuce and strawberries decided to talk to me about this library we so wanted. I met builders, librarians, doctors, and educators. Everyone wanted to be involved and volunteer to see this library through! We set a date and they all came to our school, and together we built a brand-new library.

5 Let Your School Cause Lead

Since your "why" is so important, allow it to lead every aspect of your school. This has so much to do with community empowerment because your community will follow your school cause. It is like the bow of a ship. It should be out front, pointing the way. Your school cause will speak to your community more powerfully than your beautiful school mission that is typed out, framed, and hanging on your wall. Your school cause (why) should be so visible that everyone knows it! You can test it by asking anyone about your school and why it exists. If they can't tell you within the next breath, you have work to do. The "why" is the engine that moves the school. It is the heartbeat of a school, the soul of a school.

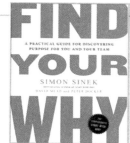

💬 FURTHERING THE CONVERSATION

Find Your Why: A Practical Guide for Discovering Purpose for You and Your Team by Simon Sinek, David Mead, and Peter Docker

If we are to profoundly change the way in which the business world works, if we help organizations create cultures in which trust and cooperation are the norm rather than the exception, if we are to build the world we imagine, we will need help. Lots of it.

The authors wrote this book to be a practical guide. A complete self-contained handbook that gives any person the pieces they need to discover and articulate their "why." They designed the book with lots of space in the margins so that you can take notes along the way. Fill in the blanks, dog-ear the pages, highlight as you go. Don't be precious about it.

Find Your Why is a journey. Though all the how-to steps may be in the book, it's going to take work and patience to really get it. Remember, this book is a guide. Follow the steps, learn the concepts, and absolutely tweak as you go to make the process your own. If you find something that works better for you, do it!

Think of this book as the gun that fires at the beginning of the race. That bang fills you with excitement and energy as you set off. But it is the lessons you will learn as you run the race—as you learn to live your "why"—that will inspire you and show you what you are capable of. And remember the most important lesson: The goal is not simply for you to cross the finish line, but to see how many people you can inspire to run with you.

Take the Why Not? Challenge: What Is Your School's "Why"?

Now it is time for you to find why your school exists. This is a deep soul-search of your school. Once it is discovered, it will cause everything else to fall into place. Take time to get quiet and answer the questions below.

1. Why does our school exist?
2. What is the purpose for all the programs, enrichment programs, and daily activities?
3. How can we let the community know about our school cause?

 REFLECTION PROMPTS

- **What is your school cause?**
- **Why do you think your school should exist?**
- **If the city wanted to tear down your school and you had to tell them why it shouldn't, what would you tell them?**

PART II
Establishing and Maintaining Successful School-Community Partnerships

Now that we have spent time talking about empowering your school community and how to do that effectively, it is time to focus on developing community partnerships. As far as I am concerned, schools cannot do all their work alone. It is not only important but essential that we be honest with our communities about needing help. Listen. To educate children is an awesome but gigantic task! What I am talking about is not mercenary at all. I did not write this book just to show educators how to get money or resources. It is about developing relationships and partnerships that create a win-win situation for both of you. This approach helped me create partnerships that have lasted for 5, 10, and 20 years! I am talking about sustainability.

The scholars who come into the school buildings now need much more. Schools need help with the execution of programs. And don't get me started on technology! With the constant changes that are happening, we need all the help we can get.

To me, there is no shortage of partnerships for every school on the planet. In my view, there are no small partners. Sometimes I think we are working too hard in education when we take on projects by ourselves that are screaming for a community partner.

Think about it. Many schools are focused on STEM, STEAM, Arts, Robotics, Culinary Arts, Medicine, Innovation, Entrepreneurship, and more. Yet, I wonder, do they have community partners helping them? I am often shocked that many of them don't. They have exhausted their budgets to pay for supplies, staffing, materials, and time. And experience is needed as well. That is where partners can come in. What an opportunity, right? They can help support the teacher. Many teachers are multitalented and can join their expertise with the partner. I remember a teacher at Morningside High School who was an awesome musician. He worked collaboratively with the Los Angeles Philharmonic and they made beautiful music together as they brought in more music enrichment programs for the school. No pun intended. That is a partnership as well.

In this section, I will endeavor to inform, reframe, and reignite your desire for community partnerships. A lot of times, I meet educators who are a bit leery of working with partners. Let me assure you, when I talk about saying yes to community partnerships, I am saying say yes to a win-win situation. Look at it this way. You are not in the back seat allowing the community partner to drive. On the contrary! You are at the wheel and your community partner is helping put gasoline in your car so you can stop running on fumes!

Educators are often amazed at the 200+ community partnerships I have been able to secure. I always let people know that it did not come without developing relationships, trust, understanding, and a hunger for more. It came only after being able to empower my community. It took me over 25 years to be able to get it right and have repeated success! It definitely wasn't done overnight, but you can do it, too. I must tell you there are times when this work will challenge you, but stay the course and say yes to community partnerships.

Be the Solution

You are the solution to your community engagement needs. Boom! This is not a one-sided deal. They need us just as much as we need them. When I finally realized this, it gave me a boldness to develop community partnerships like never before. If you see your school as their community engagement solution, you can go out there and get the partnership.

Let me use some business terms if you don't mind. Understand there are many businesses and corporate partners who genuinely want to engage their community, but they also have to. For one, it is a tax write-off, and second, it is a worthy thing to do, which is good PR for the organization. Many companies even hire people whose job it is to help them engage with their community. These positions are usually a director of community engagement, community relations, or public relations. Their job is to find worthy causes, philanthropic opportunities, and partnerships that will also benefit them in some way. Those kinds of partnerships are good for the entire community and everyone wins (Henderson, 2018; Taylor, 2016).

A Role for Business

Today, corporations speak of "Corporate Social Responsibility." CSR refers to a company's sense of responsibility toward the community and environment (both ecological and social). Harvard Business School research (2013) found that companies with more corporate social responsibility practices outperform their counterparts over time both in terms of value on the stock market and accounting performance. CSR is also an effective way to increase a company's competitive advantage.

When companies use their CSR platforms to partner with schools, they increase their presence among students, parents, school staff, and the community. This presence creates a lasting positive image that, in turn, increases a company's profits and competitive advantage.

Blair Taylor (2016) argues community engagement is not just a "nice thing to do" for businesses, but rather a "business imperative"—and should move from the philanthropic arm of the corporation and into the corporate board room. The vast and complex challenges our nation's schools now face demand a comprehensive community collaboration among all who care about our nation's children. Plus, as Taylor reminds us, the "Henry Ford model" still applies. Businesses have an incentive to invest in the workforce. They need an educated workforce to staff their jobs—and then, too, businesses are growing their own future markets. College-educated students will, on average, earn a million dollars more

> **"** The vast and complex challenges our nation's schools now face demand a comprehensive community collaboration among all who care about our nation's children. **"**

over the course of their lifetimes than their peers who don't have college degrees; what's more, college graduates have a 50% lower probability of being unemployed, promoting overall workplace stability. Why is this important for community partnership seekers? Well, if we are going to partner with businesses, we have to know how businesses think. Think about how a business workforce team can assist your scholars or bring value to your school. That is what they will be wondering, and you should be, too.

My School Pride Story

I think I should begin by sharing an unusual opportunity that came to me several years ago when I was the principal of George Carver Elementary School in Compton, California.

It's funny how life goes. Who would believe that I would be asked to be the consulting producer of an NBC reality show? It was called *School Pride*. I am still in disbelief. Let me start from the beginning of how this happened.

One year, Cheryl Hines, the actress from the popular Larry David show, *Curb Your Enthusiasm*, was a celebrity guest reader on our school campus. When she came, she saw that our playground equipment was broken and was wrapped in yellow caution tape. It troubled her and she wanted to talk to me about it.

She wanted to help us get a new one. Because of her help and the help of many of her friends in the film industry, we were able to purchase a new jungle gym with rubber matting and remodel much of the campus inside and out. The work we did got the attention of NBC,

American Airlines partnered with the Inglewood Unified School District to install playground equipment at Centinela Elementary School. They brought out dozens of their teams to make a difference for scholars.

which offered to make a show out of it. *School Pride* was a reality show that empowered communities to take charge of transforming broken schools and renovate them into real educational institutions.

We teamed up with the producers from the popular show *Extreme Home Makeover*. A team of experts motivated and led each community through the makeover process, but it was ultimately up to the scholars, teachers, and community members to execute the restoration. We ended up remodeling seven schools around the country.

The corporate partners involved were empowered to act and share their resources for several reasons. They really wanted to genuinely help the school.

School pride is the heartbeat of a school and empowers the entire community.

Partners...Not Sponsors

I choose to refer to every person or organization I work with that helps me serve children and schools as a partner. Choice of words can be very important. This is what I learned when I was starting out on my Why Not? journey. Initially, I made the mistake of calling every partner a *sponsor* or a *donor*. Even when I sent out letters asking for help or donations. I mean, that is what they were to me until I figured out that my words were sending them in a different direction.

A *sponsor* or a *donor* implies that there is money involved. It is very detached, business-related, and dry. This label did not invite them to do more than write a check, which was supposed to solve all our problems. A *partnership*, on the other hand, is based on a relationship, with give and take and both sides benefiting—a team, if you will.

Whenever I was successful with asking a business, corporation, or even a celebrity, it was because we became partners. It was something we both wanted, collaborated on, and achieved...together! If I led by asking for a donation, our relationship may well have been built on money alone. When the donation was done, so was everything else. Now, believe me, I am not saying donations are bad or people who donate don't want to build relationships. Of course we need donations, and they are always much appreciated. I am saying that it is better to seek out a partnership so everyone wins and can keep on winning!

You might be wondering, "What do they get out of it?" These same thoughts crossed my mind when I began working with large corporations or billion-dollar organizations. In my mind in the beginning, they were already winning and they needed to share their winnings with us. That is the wrong way to look at it! They are a business and every successful business grows from win after win after win. Their win may be a tax write-off or simply having a good reputation in the community because of their partnerships. Your win may be financial support or other resources the partner can provide. Whatever the win is for both of you, it is a win. The bottom line is this:

Neither of you wins unless you have a partnership. This is what you should think about first before entering into the partnership.

This is why you need to be very astute and articulate about your vision, mission, and goals. You need to know your story, your cause, and your why. Your STORY, not just your data (test scores), will be very helpful in cultivating sustainable community partnerships. Your story is where your passion lives.

Once you change your words, it will change the perspective of who you are and how you can work together. To the left are some "partnership" words that I began to use and saw immediate results with developing community partnerships.

Words to Abandon	Words to Use
sponsor	partner
need	want
work together	collaborate
your thoughts	our ideas
engage	empower
begin	launch
develop	grow
students	scholars
problem	possibility
change	innovate
donate	support
money	resources
can't	will
hope	achieve
get	secure
strategic plan	possibility plan
staff	team
dream	possibility
role model	real model

Get to Work

During one of my travels to visit schools, I met a lovely principal who could not tell me the meaning of his school's name. It took 20 minutes to find the mission and vision, and no one knew how long the school had existed. I know that if I were a potential partner, that meeting would have been over before it had started. That is a problem. If we are going to do any kind of outreach, we must first reach into our own community and find out who we are. If we don't know that, we can't determine our value and articulate that to a potential partner.

In that case, I politely let the administrator know that he had a lot of work to do. I asked him if he had called any of the local retail stores or large chains to help them. He said no. I asked if he had picked up the phone to call any local politicians to give a helping hand. He said no. I think he just wanted the community partners to find him. I quickly told him that is not how it works.

Creating effective community partnerships takes work and a lot of it. Partners don't usually go knocking on your door. It takes a leader going out into the community and making it happen. I will share more details on what kind of work is needed, but the very first thing people need to do before calling anybody is get to know their own school. It is not enough to know where you are located and your school colors. It isn't even enough to have written your single site plan, accountability plan, or strategic plan. All those are great, but what did they tell you? Where is that plan now? More than likely, it is on a shelf collecting dust. Community partners want the plan to be in you. You have to know the soul of your school and be able to bring it to the world. That is the foundation for developing community partnerships.

> **"** If we are going to do any kind of outreach, we must first reach into our own community and find out who we are. If we don't know that, we can't determine our value and articulate that to a potential partner. **"**

Make the Cold Call

I must admit, I learned most of what I know about cold calling from telemarketing jobs I had during my college years. The main thing they taught us was to be persistent and never give up. I realize that making cold calls may be challenging for some of you and you may begin shaking at the mere thought of it. Don't worry, you're not alone. This was certainly difficult for me in the beginning, until I warmed up to it.

If you're not comfortable doing it right now, you will get there, I promise. You will need to practice in front of the mirror or on the phone with a friend, but you can definitely do it. Trust me, there

is no better way to develop partnerships. Everyone wants to do it the easy way, such as by sending an email or a letter. Nope! Being more personable is the way to go. So let's get started. I want to share with you a story about when I made my first successful cold call.

My Lawry's The Prime Rib Cold Call

One evening, my family and I went to our favorite restaurant, Lawry's The Prime Rib restaurant in Beverly Hills, California. If you have ever dined at Lawry's, then you know just how grand this place is. The dining room is absolutely beautiful and the food is delicious.

Lawry's is a very swanky, expensive restaurant in Beverly Hills. Our family occasionally went there for special occasions—and this visit soon became one! We went there once when our son was very young. As we were eating, I watched him play with his food. I was sitting there wondering how many of my scholars from my school had ever had the chance to dine at Lawry's. I guessed not many. This bothered me so much that night that I had a hard time falling asleep. When I woke up the next day, I talked myself into calling the restaurant. This was a spontaneous decision and I was not sure what I was going to say, even as I dialed the phone. I am not recommending that anyone do this, but there's a lesson to be learned, so please keep reading!

> **"**I realize that making cold calls may be challenging for some of you and you may begin shaking at the mere thought of it. Don't worry, you're not alone.**"**

When the hostess answered the phone, I immediately asked for the general manager. She asked me if he was expecting my call and before I knew it, I said, "Yes." I thought he really should be expecting a call from someone, so why couldn't it have been me? The next voice I heard was the general manager. That was when I got really nervous. When he got on the line, he sounded suspicious. "Yes?" he said.

At this point, I had to think very quickly. I told him how great a time we had at his restaurant, and I wanted to call and thank him personally.

He gave a long pause, so I added that I knew a true leader was at the helm of this restaurant and it was an honor to speak to him.

Instead of quickly ending the call, he asked me to tell him a little more about myself. I told him I was a principal of a school in Compton and wondered aloud if he even knew where Compton was. He told me he knew exactly where it was, and that it was not that far away when taking the freeway.

> **As we continued to talk, I told him about my school and he appeared interested to know more. I was very surprised that he spent so much time talking to me. I then got the courage to invite him to visit our school.**

As we continued to talk, I told him about my school and he appeared interested to know more. I was very surprised that he spent so much time talking to me. I then got the courage to invite him to visit our school, whenever he had the time. Honestly, I was not expecting him to take me up on the offer. He said he would be delighted!

I remember it like yesterday. I was nervous waiting for his arrival, but excited at the same time. I was also confused because I was not sure what to do once he arrived. Then he drove up in a beautiful, shiny sports car. I ran out to personally greet him. I was in total disbelief that he was actually there. I honestly did not have a clue what to talk to him about. And then it came to me. I asked him to tell me his story. Well, even the general manager of this famous restaurant had a story that I could not believe. He told me that he didn't always have it "good." He said he didn't grow up with a silver spoon in his mouth. As a kid, he saved coins and put them in jars that he kept in his room. He learned the value of saving money, along with a strong work ethic.

He mentioned that he worked while he was in school as a dishwasher, cook, bus boy, and just about anything you can think of. He worked his way up the ladder. I know stereotypes are wrong, but I would have never thought this white, well-to-do man went through all of that. But he did.

Then it clicked! I asked him to share his story with my scholars. I wasn't sure how long he was going to stay. He smiled, nodded his head affirmatively, and said he was willing to do it. As we visited each class, his story became even more detailed and transparent. My scholars asked him so many questions, even inappropriate ones like how much money he makes. As I sat there on pins and needles, he graciously powered through them all.

Hours went by as he took time to read to some classes and have personal conversations with many of the scholars. After we ended our tour, we thanked him for his time. He looked confused and asked when we were coming to the restaurant. I said with a smile that we didn't have any money for that. We don't have a budget line for Lawry's. Then he said something to me that I never forgot. He said, "You don't need any money."

Todd Johnson,
General Manager
of Lawry's

It was at that moment that I realized the importance of the word "partner." A partner is personal. When you gain a partner, a real relationship has formed. My new partner was just as excited as we were. My staff and I took the next few weeks reviewing etiquette skills and proper attire with our fifth-grade scholars. I told them to wear church clothes, because I knew they understood that. The day arrived for us to go to the restaurant and it was great to see the scholars all dressed up. The girls had on beautiful dresses and the boys wore shirts with collars, nice shoes, and too much cologne. One of my gentlemen scholars wore a suit, hat, a cane, and no socks! His teacher and I almost could not contain ourselves and quietly chuckled. I wondered what I had started.

> **❝***It was at that moment that I realized the importance of the word 'partner.' A partner is personal. When you gain a partner, a real relationship has formed.* **❞**

As our old, yellow school bus pulled into the restaurant's parking lot, the general manager and his staff were outside waiting to greet us in full attire. My eyes began to fill with tears. One of my scholars saw the sign that read, "Closed for Private Party." He tugged on me and said, "Dr. Sanderlin, they closed." It took a minute for me to realize that we were the private party!

There was even a red carpet rolled out for us to walk on. This was the same red carpet they use for the Rose Bowl football team celebration dinner, and they used it for us. Talk about a magical moment! One of my scholars leaned over to me and whispered, "Is all of this for us?" All I could do was nod. They took us for a complete tour of the kitchen to see the large ovens that cooked the prime rib. Then they taught our scholars how to make their famous spinning bowl salad! Some of them got to wear chef coats and felt like real chefs. At the end, they brought out an ice cream sundae bar where the scholars went wild. It was hard to hold them back!

A day I will never forget. The cold call was so worth it!

That was a day we would never, ever forget. And over the next eight years, we were invited back and hundreds of scholars got the chance to experience what I experienced with my family that night for dinner. The general manager was a real partner. He came to our school time and time again to read to the scholars and attend other events at other schools within our district.

Now, this was an unusual situation and I am not expecting you to always get these kinds of partnerships. Heck, I did not have many like this myself. However, I hope you get the picture. If I had not taken time to make that cold call, I would not have this story to tell you now.

I hope my experience helped you realize the importance of making cold calls. The most important thing is knowing what you want to say and how much time you have to say it in. In my experience, you don't have much time. What I know is that once you get your potential partner on the phone, you have exactly 10 seconds (or less) to make something good happen!

The 10-Second Script

You might have heard about the infamous 30-second elevator speech. This is not it! In this era, the concept of time has changed. Even 30 seconds is a long time today! We don't realize it, but think about it: one alligator, two alligator, three alligator...get the picture? Most people I meet don't have 30 seconds to give anymore, especially CEOs and general managers. Time is money, as they say! If you can't hook them in 10 seconds, then your time may have run out. This is when you have to sit and be quiet, because you have to think deeply about what you will say.

Time Yourself

If you are like me, you need to time yourself. I have a tendency to talk too much and too long and not let the other person get a word in edgewise. Timing yourself when you talk will help you master the 10-second script. Make an outline for yourself so you can use it to practice while you are driving, walking in the park, or even washing the dishes. Use a stopwatch so you can get it to precision! I can honestly say that my 10-second script was perfected in my car and in the shower.

66 The most important thing is knowing what you want to say and how much time you have to say it in. 99

Once you feel confident, start practicing your 10-second script every day and everywhere. Remember, if you can hook them in first 10 seconds, they will give you more seconds and you will be on your way to developing a new partner. The clock is ticking!

Beware of the Gatekeeper

There is always a gatekeeper in every business, corporation, or chain of stores. Their job is to screen every caller, even individuals seeking partnerships. You have to realize that businesses receive all kinds of calls every day. As educators, we get those calls, too.

Every gatekeeper is different. Some of them can be pretty tough, while others have a sweet, unassuming voice. Remember, that cute voice is still a gatekeeper and their number one job is to keep the gate closed! Don't forget that. You have to find a way to break through.

Don't be surprised at all the obstacles and hurdles that are purposely set up for you. Those hoops and barriers are there for a reason, particularly when you start calling the big corporations. Partnerships take work and that includes working with the gatekeeper.

I actually became friends with many of the gatekeepers I have met throughout my partnership quest. They helped me get to the person I needed to speak with and were very instrumental in helping me launch my partnerships. So make sure you are always nice and polite with them. They could be the reason you land the partnership or not.

I have found gatekeepers to be very helpful when I was polite to them and took their advice. They will ask you the nature of your call because that is their job. This is where you want to be honest and respectful. They will either connect you to the boss or their representative. Either will do. I will tell you a secret. If you are nice to them, it will help you in the long run. I made a practice of sending them an email, card, or flowers for helping me get through. Whatever you decide to do, think about ways you can show your appreciation. It will be remembered.

Let me share with you some lessons I learned and action steps so you can be successful with cold calls, too. Let's get started!

Action Steps for Making Cold Calls

1 Make a List of Your Community Partners

Think about what businesses, people, and influencers you want to contact. Start by making a list and keeping it nearby. You will be surprised by the many people, leaders, and businesses that you come in contact with on a daily basis. Keep your list handy and more importantly, visible. The names of companies and corporations on this list will begin to beckon you. This list will be a road map and a reminder of your quest to make the outreach. Understand that if you don't call, you may never meet otherwise. Then you will have lost the opportunity to make a real impact for your scholars. That alone should motivate you!

2 Stay Focused

My dad taught me this trick when he was on a mission to purchase his first income property. I used to ride in his car and see a note he taped on his dashboard that said, "Buy property, buy property, buy property!" It served as a constant reminder for him and kept him focused even while going to work. I can remember when he actually did buy the property and we knew it was that note that kept him determined to do so. The same is true for you. Post a note on your refrigerator door, bathroom mirror, or in your car that says, "Call a business, call a business, call a business!"

3 Create a System for Yourself

Do you know your local religious leaders, politicians, store owners, CEOs, or civic leaders of organizations? Work at becoming acquainted with everyone as much as possible. Create a system that works for you and call them. This is what worked for me. I would identify three to five businesses to call each week. This list

Community Partner List

Keeping a list nearby when making outreach calls will help you keep note of your successes and next steps. Post this list somewhere you will see it each day. This will motivate you to stay on the path! I like to use a simple legend for the status column.

Example: LM – left message, CB – call back, NA – no answer, TD – touchdown.

Name	Company	Email	Phone	Status

To download a simple template you can use, go to scholastic.com/WhyNotResources.

helped me stay on track and monitor my progress. It was very gratifying to know I made attempts to reach out, even if I got rejections or just left messages. I would use a system and write simple notes in the margin like CB (call back), LM (left message), or FU (follow up).

4 Do Your Homework

Doing my homework on a company or business I wanted to call helped me be a lot more effective when I reached out to them. With the help of social media, you can easily find out all you need about an organization, including names of people and more.

You want to know something about the organization's history. Take time to browse their website and take notes. You will immediately begin to see commonalities between the both of you and opportunities for possible partnerships. Find out what you can about their mission, vision, and core beliefs. When you call, you will want to know a few substantial points about their organization. They will be impressed by your knowledge.

Believe me, your potential partner will also do his or her fair share of homework on you and your school, so make sure your social, professional, and personal media channels are current and appropriate. There is nothing worse than having old or outdated information in the public eye. I cringe every time I drive by a school that says "Happy Halloween" in March. Get yourself ready before your potential partner does his or her homework on you so he or she will be able to see what your school is all about.

5 Practice Your Message

I was terrible at cold calling when I first started. My voice rattled and I was extremely nervous. Sometimes I forgot who I was calling. That's why it is important to practice! Your voice, tone, and personality matter a lot, especially on a cold call. Practice alone and

Action Steps

with a friend. I learned this the hard way when I saw partnership opportunities float by as I fumbled over my words or just sounded robotic. I didn't take the time to write it out, practice what I would say, or master my message.

When speaking to a potential partner, he or she needs to hear your vision and passion come out of you authentically, and this will take practice. The leader must breathe life into his or her vision (Kouzes & Posner, 1987). This may be a good time to reflect on whether your vision is alive and well or dead on arrival (DOA). If it is, give it CPR and resuscitate that thing before you make the call. You simply have to practice navigating through the rough terrain until you reach a smooth altitude at the top!

Your cold call could make the difference between a plan and a partnership.

6 Be Authentic

Developing your message with authenticity takes time but is required if you are going to be successful with cold calling potential partners. Your authenticity and even mistakes will be warmly received. Actually, being honest and humble is refreshing to most business leaders and CEOs because they are used to people cold calling to sell them something. Your potential partner wants to know the real you, your dreams and struggles. It is okay to tell the partner about your school's needs and goals. That is real stuff and can open up avenues for partnership opportunities.

7 Seek Feedback

Feedback is most powerful when it is timely, specific to established criterion, and corrective in nature. We all need feedback on our message, voice tone, body language, facial expressions, and how we come across. I had a trusted critic who would tell me if

I was talking too fast (which I did a lot), too much (that, too), or not enough. Sometimes we are just not aware of these faults, so it behooves us to find a trusted critic to tell us the truth. Getting real feedback on these areas could help you develop countless partnerships!

Roland Barth (1991) says little will change unless we change ourselves. If you are willing to make some tweaks and changes along the way, then you will grow and your partnerships will, too! I can't tell you how many times I've had to change my cold call approaches. Sometimes I learned the hard way when the prospective partner never called back. This may happen to you as well, but allow it to help you reflect so you can be better the next time.

8 Don't Take Rejection Personally

Whenever I was rejected or even hung up on, I did not take it personally and neither should you! As I made cold calls, I decided to make a game out of it until I got a commitment from somebody. I was looking for a Yes in a sea of Nos. When I took on that attitude and persistence, community partners began to respond and come on board with our school. The same will happen for you. Remember, each rejection will build your confidence, stamina, and character. Look at it as your way of practicing.

9 Go to the Top

Going to the top has always been my saving grace and maximized time in launching a partnership. You want to talk to the person who is in charge, by any means necessary! He or she is the one who makes the decisions. By hook or crook (mostly by hook), do whatever you can to get the boss on the line. This is important because if you can make a believer out of him or her, you have already begun to pave the path to your new partnership!

Action Steps

Sample Gatekeeper Script

Gatekeeper: Hello, how may I help you?

You: Hello, how are you? (Wait for an answer—
sometimes the person wants to comment about
themselves or the weather. If they do, roll with it.)
Well, I am calling for your general manager.
(Use that person's name if you have it.)

Gatekeeper: May I ask who is calling and the purpose
of the call?

You: Sure. I am Dr. Jackie and I am the principal
of _____ .

Gatekeeper: Are they expecting your call?

You (two options): Yes. (Don't be afraid to say yes, because
you are a community partner and all corporations
are seeking community engagement. It's a stretch,
but if you have the guts, go for it! If they get on the
phone, you can say that. I have used this approach
a lot and it has worked! Some even laughed about
it when I told them.)

Or:

No, but I would really like to pay them a
compliment, which is why I took the time to call.
It will only take a minute.

(Either approach has worked for me. It all depends on the
gatekeeper, the moment, the timing, and you.)

Sample 10-Second Script

Hello. I am _____ and I am the principal of _____ school in
_____. Thank you for taking my call. I just wanted to personally
reach out and thank you for the work you provide the community.
I would love to hear your story.

(I know that seems very short, but that is the point. It leaves room
for them to share their story. People want to be recognized.
When they finish, be sure to give them an invitation to come
to your school.)

Sample Partnership Outreach Email

**(Sometimes, they will ask you to send an email instead.
You can use this one as a model.)**

Hello. I am _____ and I am the principal of _____ school in
_____. I called you today to thank you for your work in the
community and wanted to invite you to my school so you can
share your leadership story with my scholars. I am always seeking
to bring REAL models (not just ROLE models) to our scholars so

they can be inspired by their
journeys. I know you are super
busy, but if you could carve
out a little time to come to our
campus, we would be most
grateful. Please let me know
which date is good for you.

Action Steps

FURTHERING THE CONVERSATION

Improving Schools Through Community Engagement: A Practical Guide for Educators

by Kathy Gardner Chadwick

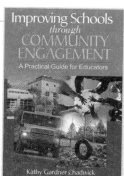

Americans see public schools as a critical community resource and rank education as a priority second only to the economy. How can educators harness this public interest in education to bring parents, families, and communities to action for our schools? *Improving Schools Through Community Engagement* addresses these questions and more.

Involvement of family and community members has a significant impact on student achievement. This handy resource provides a framework that education leaders can use in designing and implementing initiatives to more effectively engage the public by:

- Framing a clear focus for community engagement.
- Identifying and including representatives from each diverse constituency group.
- Developing an understanding of the varied perspectives of these groups.
- Presenting strategies to encourage constituent involvement and action.

The energy of parents, teachers, and communities working together starts small and spreads over time. If everyone gets involved, the possibilities for action are limitless!

Take the Why Not? Challenge: Make Some Cold Calls!

This week, make a list of 10 companies/organizations to cold call. Then call them!

1. Write out a draft of your 10-second script.
2. Practice it in the mirror and with a trusted critic.
3. Prepare further talking points.
4. Get past any fears, use your call list, and get going!

> ### 🔲 REFLECTION PROMPTS
> - **What will you say when you call?**
> - **Do you have your list ready?**
> - **Who is your trusted critic to practice your cold calling with?**
> - **What can you do to be more authentic?**

Prepare for Your First Meeting

Congratulations! You have been invited to a real sit-down meeting with a potential partner after your cold call! There is no way around it. You will be looking in his or her face and he or she will be looking at yours. This is your moment to shine, bond, and lock it down. You want to think about what you will wear, what you will say, and how you will say it.

If you have made it this far, congratulations! This first meeting can be a game changer, even if your meeting is online. It is a meeting that has the potential of going left or right. This meeting can be the

beginning of a beautiful partnership, so let's look a little more deeply at how you should handle it as I share my first meeting with the L.A. Rams.

That organization has done so much good work at schools all over Los Angeles, from reading to scholars, installing playground equipment, creating maker spaces, hosting Play 60 sports events, and providing free tickets for educators, scholars, and their families to attend their games. They even provided paid internships for high schoolers in Inglewood one summer. These are the kinds of partnership opportunities that can be started in your sit-down meeting. Let me share a few more experiences.

My Partnership With the L.A. Rams

When I was working for the Inglewood Unified School District, there was an excitement in the air because the Los Angeles Rams were coming to Inglewood to build a brand-new stadium! Everyone was talking about it; it was the chatter of most people's conversation: "How is the weather, did you hear about the Rams coming?" "How is your family? You know the Rams are coming, right?" No one could stop talking about it. As the Executive Director of School and Community Relations at the time, it was my job to develop community partnerships and empower the local community. I was more than excited to meet with Molly Higgins, the Vice President of Community Affairs for the L.A. Rams. Below is a list of partnership activities we did together that might inspire you in your next partnership meeting.

- During the team's first year back home in Los Angeles in 2016, Rams players, cheerleaders, and front office staff built a playground for Woodworth Elementary School in Inglewood as part of the team's Annual Community Improvement Project.
- In 2017, the Los Angeles Rams and the California Milk Advisory Board presented Inglewood Unified School District with a $10,000 grant to support healthy eating and physical activity programs for schools within the district.

- As part of the Rams' 2017 Cleats for Character program, the team donated more than 100 pairs of athletic shoes to Inglewood High School and Morningside High School.

- In October 2017, Rams players, cheerleaders, and staff beautified Inglewood Unified School District's Warren Lane Elementary School campus with murals and landscaping.

- In partnership with the Inglewood Police Department, the Rams invited families with special needs children on a shopping spree at Target to purchase items on their holiday wish lists.

- In 2018, the Rams teamed up with the Ross Initiative in Sports for Equality (RISE) to pilot a season-long leadership and community-building program featuring Morningside High School in Inglewood and Oaks Christian High School in Westlake Village. The collaboration was designed to harness the unifying power of sports and build relationships between two Los Angeles–area high school football teams with a cross-section of races and socioeconomic backgrounds.

- For the team's 2018 and 2019 Training Camps, the Rams worked with LA Promise Fund to customize an internship program for recent high school graduates from Inglewood Unified School District to provide deserving high school students a chance to work in dynamic career fields through paid internship opportunities.

- During the 2018 season, the L.A. Rams and L.A. Chargers teamed up to surprise two Inglewood high schools with new football uniforms. Each team donated $10,000 for a total of 100

Molly and I had big dreams from the start. The L.A. Rams is making an impact on and off the field for youth all over Los Angeles County.

new uniforms and footballs to the varsity football programs of Inglewood High School and Morningside High School.

- Los Angeles Rams cornerback Marcus Peters surprised 400 students with new backpacks filled with school supplies at Century Park Elementary School in Inglewood.

- As part of the "Read Across America Day" celebration in March of 2018, the Rams delivered books to Claude Hudnall and Frank D. Parent elementary schools in Inglewood to enrich their classroom libraries.

- In celebration of Earth Day in April 2018, Rams front-office staffers worked with LA Conservation Corps to plant trees on streets near the site of the L.A. Stadium and Entertainment District at Hollywood Park in Inglewood.

Excited to be facilitating a conversation between educators and potential partners. This was professional development renewed!

- On June 1, 2019, the Los Angeles Rams hosted a Community Day in Inglewood that featured a free, coed football clinic that was open to the public and a donation that provided local youth and their families with gear worn by Rams players and coaches, such as cleats, hats, shirts, pants, etc.

- In June 2019, the Rams committed to refurbish the grass football field at Morningside High School, which will serve as the home field for both Inglewood high school football programs.

- Also in June, the Rams engaged Inglewood Parks & Rec Flag Football League to rename the league the "Inglewood Rams," with each team named after current Rams players. Officers with the Inglewood Police Department will also be joining the efforts and will serve as coaches/mentors for the 11- to 14-years-old teams to continue bridging the gaps between law enforcement and communities of color.

> **66** *It is not about having all the answers, it's about sharing a common belief that great things can happen when potential partners sit down and meet.* **99**

- On October 18, 2019, the Los Angeles Rams legend Ron Brown attended a high school football matchup at Morningside High School in Inglewood to recognize their varsity football coach as the Rams' "Coach of the Week." The Morningside head coach received a $2,000 grant from the Los Angeles Rams and an additional $1,000 in Gatorade products.

As you can see, we were able to accomplish so much from one successful and relaxing sit-down meeting and so can you. It is not about having all the answers, it's about sharing a common belief that great things can happen when potential partners sit down and meet. To this day, we continue to meet about more partnership opportunities.

The WME Sit-Down

"How much paper do you have?" This was the question I asked Sarah from WME (William Morris Endeavor) during our first meeting. She was the director of their foundation. She wanted me to tell her what our school needed and wanted. I knew the answer to that question well because it was something I thought about a lot. I was ready! WME was looking for a school with a passionate leader whom they could partner with. They were interested in developing a partnership that would provide sustainable support for youth as they matriculated all the way to college (K–12).

When I look back, I am so happy I showed my passion during that first meeting. For me, I didn't think of it as passion—I simply wanted to do something special because my scholars deserved it. I was tired of waiting for the state, federal government, or even my own school budget to handle it.

Lucky for us, WME felt my passion and selected our school to partner with. We ended up taking some massive leaps that could never have been done without them. We were able to completely remodel the school inside and out, add new playground equipment, art classes, musical instruments, enrichment programs, summer programs, mentoring programs, a learning garden, library books, field trips, basketball courts, exterior lighting, new bathrooms—the list literally goes on! I run out of breath every time I tell people about this partnership. Can you believe it? We were even able to get our school bathrooms remodeled by the owner of the Boston Celtics, because of our partnership with WME!

We also installed a full-size tennis court! I remember they even painted it the official U.S. Open blue. We were the only elementary school in our community with a tennis court. Then we got a nine-hole putting green installed with golf instructors and equipment, all free of charge! WME also introduced us to Food Network celebrity chef Giada de Laurentiis. She had some pretty big dreams herself. She helped us build a gorgeous learning garden. Our scholars loved growing different vegetables and harvesting them. Teachers would even have classes out there. It was a sight to behold. Over my 20 years in Compton, I had not seen that before. WME made a huge impact at my school and for the Compton Unified School District. They were partners who wanted to genuinely see the scholars they worked with go to college some day. This is a partnership that lasted for over 10 years and counting! You can't tell me that a grant would have done the same.

Digital Hollywood

During the past 25 years, Victor Harwood has developed and produced over 200 conferences and events for artists, professionals, and top executives. Mr. Harwood is considered a leading authority on the convergence of the entertainment and technology industries, organizing such conferences as Digital Hollywood. I am honored to be part of Digital Hollywood's annual gathering that puts educators in the same room as filmmakers, digital leaders, and celebrities to see what partnerships can be formed. The Digital Hollywood experience brought professional development to a new world!

Link the Partnership to Learning

As educators, our job is to always link our partnerships to learning. Whenever I meet with a potential partner, that is always the first topic of discussion. Everything else flows from there. Our overall goal is to increase student achievement, access, and opportunities for our scholars. Be clear about that and repeat it as often as necessary! By doing so, you will create a visual for them so they can ask you that beautiful question, "How can we help you with that?"

When a partnership is linked to learning, partners become empowered to cooperatively work with you toward your academic goals. As William Glasser (1998) notes, "Learning together as a member of a small learning team is much more need-satisfying, especially to the needs for power and belonging, than learning individually" (p. 48). Your community partner will become a part of your professional learning community.

The Partnership Tango Dance

I love to dance, so this analogy is my favorite! You may be arriving to the meeting as strangers, but expect to leave as partners. This is how you must think. The first meeting is a dance, and you need to know the steps. If you dance too fast, you leave your partner behind. If you dance too slow, they leave you and look for another partner. If you are dancing in step, then both of you are in harmony and neither of you is stepping on the other's feet. That's the kind of successful partnership meeting that you want. Now, if this meeting goes well, you will be invited back for a second one where others may be involved. If that happens, you are on your way to Partnershipville, my friend!

Action Steps for Preparing for Your First Sit-Down Meeting

1 Meet in a Comfortable, Relaxed Environment

If you are asked to select the meeting spot, choose carefully. You will be judged by which one you choose. I would certainly stay away from night clubs, parks, or loud places. I always say that food is the universal language, so choose a restaurant and you won't go wrong. I suggest keeping a handy-dandy list of quaint local eateries. You want the ambiance to be comfortable so both of you can be relaxed. Food lays a great foundation for partnerships to grow. If they choose the place, accept wherever it is. They may want to meet at their place of business, which is an excellent way to learn more about them. Many potential partners are willing to open their doors so they can show you what they are doing.

2 Introduce Yourself and Smile

Always bring a welcoming smile. Remember, they will not just be partnering with your school, they will be going into partnership with YOU! This is something I actually practice in the mirror. I want to make sure my smile is genuine, and I want to know what I look like when I smile. Try it. It will feel weird at first, but it's worth knowing. A good friend of mine spent over $5,000 on his teeth so he could be more presentable. He is a musician and performer and said his job has a lot of to do

with his face, so he had to get it done. While some of you reading this may think that is a lot of money, he said he could have spent it on other things he didn't need, so he invested in his smile. He wasn't happy with it before and now he proudly shows his pearly whites wherever he goes!

3 Remember That the Meeting Is an "Interview"

Before you go on an interview, you usually think about what you will wear and say. This is also a meeting where you want to present your best self. As the saying goes, nothing beats a first impression, so don't take this initial meeting lightly. Think of the sit-down meeting as an interview...because it is! While you all may be eating and having a good time, they are evaluating whether this is a good partnership or not. You should be doing the same.

4 Dress for Success

Yes, what you wear matters. Business-casual is the safest bet. Steer away from wearing extremely loud colors, perfume, or cologne. You want the focus to be on your plans to partner, not your clothes or hairstyle.

5 End With Commas, Not Periods

These conversations are so critical, you have to be careful not to cut them off too soon. The relationship you are forming needs ample time to mature. You can make a critical mistake by ending it with a period or walking off without discussing next steps.

This very thing happened when I connected a multimillion-dollar corporation with a colleague. I thought this partnership would be a good match. I knew what the school needed and what the partnership could look like. The principal met with them and was very excited about the possibilities, and the partner was, too! But then there was no follow-up by the principal. That was it—nothing else, zip! The CEO called me and was confused. He said, "Hey Jackie, she must not have been very interested." I asked why, and he said she never asked us to meet, have lunch, or take any additional steps. Don't make that mistake.

6 Leave Your Agenda at Home

Be prepared, but don't bring a printed agenda. It looks kind of hokey and premeditated. One time I went to a partnership sit-down meeting with my supervisor and she whipped out five copies of an agenda. The potential partners across the table looked like they wanted to run. This was a huge partnership that would have served every school within our district, so I think she wanted to be really prepared. After a couple of those meetings, the constant agendas ended up scaring them off and the partnership never manifested. From that point on, I decided to never do that. Sometimes you can learn from other people's mistakes. You can bring a notepad to take notes, but it is rarely a good idea to sit in front of them with an open laptop. That will act as a barrier and keep you from developing a bond. What we want here is to have an open conversation.

Action Steps

7 Relax

When you have your first meeting, let the conversation develop at its own pace. Don't rush it. If you relax, they will relax. Don't arrive too wound up or stiff. This will cause your potential partners to feel uncomfortable. Do some deep breathing before arriving and calm yourself down. Relax, turn down the heat, and let the conversation cook like a slow-cooked pot roast.

 FURTHERING THE CONVERSATION

The Coaching Partnership: Collaboration for Systemic Change
by Rosemarye Taylor and Carol Chanter

When teachers, coaches, mentors, and administrators successfully work together in a collaborative coaching partnership, everyone's effectiveness increases—and student achievement grows. *The Coaching Partnership* provides educators with a unique perspective and approach to instructional coaching centered on mutual and reciprocal accountability for continuous improvement. This essential resource provides the guidance and tools educators need to implement a coaching partnership system in their schools and achieve their ultimate goal: improved student learning outcomes.

Drawing on their extensive experience and years of research, the authors identify all the necessary components for a successful coaching partnership, and show teachers, coaches, mentors, and administrators how to:

- Optimize coaching partnerships with clearly defined processes and roles.
- Foster a culture of generative thinking to encourage learning, inquiry, and lasting change.
- Build trust to create successful collaborative, equitable relationships.
- Use frameworks to implement an evidence-based approach to coaching.
- Commit to an effective coaching system that makes improved performance last.

Take the Why Not? Challenge: Plan a First Meeting!

- Identify a business partner and contact him or her this week.
- Ask to meet with him or her at their convenience but gently press him or her for a meeting date.
- Review the talking points and sentence starters you came up with for the meeting.
- Block out a couple of hours so you can get there on time and have a good conversation.
- Breathe, look at yourself in the mirror, smile, and develop the partnership. Good luck!

REFLECTION PROMPTS

Think about how you can link a partner to your learning goals.

- **Do face-to-face meetings make you nervous? If so, why?**
- **How can you turn a cold call into a first meeting?**
- **What talking points will you use in your first sit-down meeting?**

Follow Up With Your Partners

I can remember when I visited one of the schools in my district for a principal's meeting. I was enamored at the beauty—the trees, benches, flowers, and murals. I even saw people (not employees of the school) who were planting flowers and tending to the garden outside of the main office. I saw others sprucing up the murals. I was in awe of what was going on. It's safe to say that this principal was a major inspiration to me in terms of developing community partnerships. I remember asking her how she was able to make all of this happen at her school and she said, "Partnerships! And I follow up with them regularly."

She told me that she had always focused on creating partnerships but found that following up with them often was even more important than establishing the partnership in the first place. I took a seat and asked her to explain that to me. She said that regardless of what her schedule looked like, she always made time to call a partner back, meet with the partner, and thank him or her. She said she sent thank-you cards and photos throughout the year. She reminded me that she did this quickly so she would not forget and that they always appreciated it. She taught me a valuable lesson about the importance of following up with my partners.

When I started out creating partnerships, I remembered the lesson. I wanted my partners to feel good, vested, and part of our solution. In the beginning, I would flop at it because I let too much time go by. Other times, I would forget to call back. So I made up the 24-hour follow-up method for myself. I made a deal with myself to make sure to follow up with a partner within 24 hours and it always got done after that. This was more than a timing thing, it became a good practice for me. Since I made a point to respond with a phone call, email, or text, I

Providing workshops to educators on how to work with their partners is rewarding for me. Here I am talking to educators from Lathrop Intermediate School in the Santa Ana Unified School District.

was able to remember details and the proper responses to share with them. I also knew that it got done. The worst thing to ever do is leave a partner hanging. We are so busy and so many things can easily get in the way. It is not like we mean to not respond, but it happens. In order to keep this from happening, I suggest you adopt my policy of following up within 24 hours. It will help you stay on track and it will make your partner feel appreciated.

Now, following up should not feel like homework or a severe task. What I mean is simply taking a few minutes to send an email, phone call, text message, or pictures. If you like sending letters, feel free to go old school. It is up to you. The point is to just do it. I think you get the message. These follow-up efforts don't have to be long, arduous, or perfect either. Remember, it is the thought that counts.

> **❝I wanted my partners to feel good, vested, and part of our solution. ❞**

What helps me is keeping brief notes of what the partner did and how he or she impacted my students and school overall. I love storytelling and creating photos that tell a story about what he or she did as well. It is more authentic and real. Make following up a priority because there are some consequences to not following up that I have experienced as well.

Whenever I failed to follow up, the relationship with the partner was negatively affected. By not following up, the partner didn't know how I felt or the impact he or she really made. And when I let too much time go by, it kind of felt like an afterthought. One of the worst things that happened was when the partner would reach out to see if I was displeased somehow with his or her service or if we were okay. I would have to apologize and blame my hectic schedule. Listen, don't beat yourself up when you go past 24 hours. I just want you to be mindful that time is of the essence, but whether it is 24, 48, or 72 hours later, it does not matter. Just follow up! Better late than never!

Now here are some action steps that helped me achieve efficiency and authenticity in all my follow-up experiences.

Action Steps for Following Up With Partners

1 Send an Email

I know this sounds simple, but you want to take this one seriously. Your emails can be general in nature and provide a warm thank you or you can take the time to record some detailed accounts and share reactions. Sometimes I would even share what others have said and attach photos. These emails are very much welcomed. Use the email as an opportunity to copy others who were involved. It is a great tool to communicate and share quick thoughts.

2 Text

Well, we all know how fast texting is. I would use this method to send a quick note of thanks the same day as the partnership event just to make sure I said something. I would usually follow up with a more formal email and attach any pictures as well. Texting would provide an instant response as well as let them know how much I appreciated their partnership. I could also upload any pics I took and immediately thank them. Try it!

3 Letters

I am kind of old school when it comes to letters and yes, I still send them. I have been known to send cards, handwritten letters, and notes in the mail. This one usually blows them away. I know writing letters may be a stretch for some of you, but give it a try.

4 Communicate Regularly

Just start communicating with your partners on a regular basis. You can share information like newsletters, updates, and events. This is one way I was able to make quick connections, and the partnership network became a team for good. They will stay updated on your school and any community partnership projects. When you do this, you will start to empower your partners and they will want to keep it going. You will be surprised how your network gets stronger and grows roots within your community.

5 Make Presentations/Updates

It is always a good idea to find opportunities to acknowledge the partnership work that is taking place on your campus.
I did this on many occasions. I would attend their all-company or board of directors meetings and give an update. It would allow me to acknowledge their good work and meet others from the corporation. There is nothing like hearing from the end user. Remember, they are reporting on your partnership to their teams, and hearing authentic feedback will strengthen your corporate partnership.

6 Phone Calls

This is the most personal way to communicate. Nothing beats the human voice. I know we live in a digital age, but please try and squeeze in some phone calls if you can. It's so uncommon it will be welcomed. Now if the person you are calling is not

Hosting the Dr. Jackie STEM/STEAM Innovation Forum at the Skirball Cultural Center in Los Angeles, California.

available, leave a voicemail, and this will still count as a legitimate follow-up. They will be able to hear the appreciation and zeal in your voice that no text or email can convey. If you are nervous about doing this, just take a few moments to breathe, practice what you will say, and go for it. They will not forget it. In fact, it could lead to a new conversation of more partnership opportunities.

7 Contact the Media

One sure way to follow up is to invite the media to create a story. By doing this, you are accomplishing several things. First of all, good public relations is what every school and business needs. This will provide local or even national headlines for your partnership. Your partner will also be happy because it shines a positive light on his or her corporation as well. All in all, everyone wins. Keep a list handy of several news reporters so you can give them some lead time. They are usually excited to get a good community interest story.

FURTHERING THE CONVERSATION

School, Family, and Community Partnerships: Your Handbook for Action
by Joyce L. Epstein and Associates

How can teachers and administrators be prepared to create partnerships with families and communities? Well-known and respected author Joyce Epstein updates her acclaimed *School, Family, and Community Partnerships* to reflect the past 10 years of study and advancements. New readings address this growing field and offer expanded consideration of district leadership and its impact on school programs. Epstein contends it is now possible to prepare teachers and administrators with a solid base of knowledge on partnerships. Theoretical perspectives and results from research and development can and should be shared with educators. As partners, parents and teachers share responsibility for the education and development of their children. Common messages and collaborative activities of home and school help to promote student success, prevent problems, and solve those that arise. Epstein provides the material needed to help current educators and educators in training think about, talk about, and then act to develop comprehensive programs of school, family, and community partnerships. This is a definitive resource both in and out of the classroom with comments, discussion questions, activities, and field experiences in each of the chapters.

Take the Why Not? Challenge:
Follow Up With a Partner

Think about a partner you need to follow up with, whether it was a while ago or very recently, and do it. Choose one of my methods and feel free to use the talking points I have provided at scholastic.com/ WhyNot Resources to reach out to him or her. You will be glad you did, and the partner will, too! It can either prolong a new partnership or resurface an old one.

 REFLECTION PROMPTS

- **Which follow-up method fits you best?**
- **Which partner do you need to follow up with immediately?**
- **Whom can you call now?**
- **What is hindering you from following up at all?**

Why Not? Challenge #9
Explore Funding Opportunities

As an educator, I know everyone wants to know how to secure financial support for the things your school needs. I get it. Let's face it, money makes things happen. All our schools could use more resources, and community partners can be an excellent source of support.

No one should feel ashamed to admit that. It takes money to be able to get many of the things our schools need and the reality is that our budgets are never big enough. So we have to be thoughtful in what we decide to purchase year after year. And we know these

purchases are usually shared with the collective voices of others who help determine what our priorities need to be. Many of these layers can cause administrative fatigue and seeming impossibilities even though we have site plans, strategic plans, and goals.

But there are ways to increase funding streams and to create more opportunities to support your school through community partnerships. In addition to the "traditional" ways of bringing in funds, I would like to announce that community partnerships and philanthropic organizations can help you do the same, and in some cases, help you bring in even more.

> 66 *There are ways to increase funding streams and to create more opportunities to support your school through community partnerships.* 99

When I was a principal, my school was fortunate to be provided with resources and cold hard cash from community partnerships. That was a huge help in many ways. We also received in-kind gifts, materials, supplies, time, and much more. Some of you reading this book have received gifts of financial support from partners. For some of you, this may be a new concept and it is your goal to make it happen.

Whoever you are, I want to show you how to start a flow of financial support and keep you safe and protected while doing so. School districts are tricky, political spaces. You have to make sure you are following protocol so you don't get into any trouble. I will tell you right now that when you begin to get checks, there is a process that you must follow where you work. I implore you to find out how your district handles financial gifts. You also want to know how the check can be placed in an account that is earmarked for your school. When you start developing partnerships with financial benefits, everyone wants a piece of the pie. Trust me, I had to watch my budget and follow the guidelines set up in my own district.

Remember, there is nothing wrong with this. This is not a mercenary intention. I have learned that part of developing community partnerships was to help them invest in good causes, like my school. As I have said before, they are honestly looking for great causes and funding opportunities, and genuinely want to help schools like yours. You will also learn that some businesses only want to support you financially. They may not have the time or the bandwidth to do more. I have run into many organizations who have told me this. That is okay because they are still a community partner and should be referred to as one. They are not a sponsor or a donor (as I said earlier in this book), but a community partner who found their way to support. Sometimes that is done strictly with money.

In this chapter, I would like to show you how to keep those financial streams open, how to broaden them for sustainability, how to use the funding with the right intentions, and how to stay out of political traps that could be detrimental to your community partnership success.

Action Steps for Exploring Funding Opportunities

1 Never Ask for Money, Because You Just Might Get It!

This is what I know for sure—money should not be your primary goal when developing community partnerships. It just shouldn't! This is difficult for some educators who work in under-resourced communities to understand. I made this mistake when I asked WalMart for $10,000 and they gave it to me. After that, I never heard from them again. WalMart is a billion-dollar corporation! That was a drop in the bucket for them. I give myself credit for getting it, but I wished I had allowed them to tell me what they wanted to give. Who knows what they would have said.

My focus should have been on developing a relationship with them so they could become a partner in education with me. But that was a lesson I had to learn so I could be able to tell you and everyone else about it. Don't make the same mistake.

2 Understand Financial Gifts

It took me a while to understand this. Financial gifts are not grants or a scholarship. Those are different. When my school was getting so much money and financial gifts, I thought it was like a gift. According to the dictionary, a gift is property, money, or assets that one person transfers to another while receiving nothing or less than fair market value in return. Under certain circumstances, the IRS collects a tax on gifts. Many or all community partners who provided you with a check will receive a tax write-off. They report their financial gifts to the Internal Revenue Service (IRS).

Everything that is given to your school does have a dollar sign attached to it, even though it comes to you as "free." When businesses provide these financial donations, it is part of their annual budget and there is a line item for that.

Partners can contribute dollars or in-kind support in the form of access to family programs, and more (Blank, Jacobson, Melville, and Pearson, 2010). Corporations and philanthropic organizations usually seek out charitable opportunities to "plant a seed" that can reap benefits over many years. Your school could be the soil for their seed giving. Why not?

3 Know How Much You Need

If what you want costs money, be prepared to share with your partners the costs involved. Some community partners have set aside funding to do just that and schools need the assistance of community partners to help offset the costs they incur on a daily basis. It also helps fill in the gaps where their local, state, and federal funding streams run dry.

Knowing what you want is more important than knowing what you need with community partners.

Many partners would ask me to define my ask to a specific number. This may happen to you. This caused me some anxiety because I was not sure if my number was too big and would turn them off. Don't worry about that. Be honest and tell them. Your specificity will allow them to move quicker on your behalf. You can't be scared of the cost of something. I mean, that is what it costs! Be upfront and let them know. Listen, you can't win them all. If the partner realizes they can't pay for it, they will tell you or move on. That is okay. But you have to be ready to answer the question if it comes up. Also realize that they are not the only community partner you will have. There will always be more opportunities, and every partnership is different.

While you don't want to limit what they give, they will need to know a close ballpark figure. Have this information ready so when they ask you, you can access it immediately. Who knows? They may give you more than what you need.

Do your due diligence by getting several quotes on how much what you want will cost and present those to your community partner. It's a good idea to show them that you did your homework. Always choose the most reasonable figure for what you want. Remember, businesses are successful for a reason: They look for the best price on everything! Your ability to do the same will create a lot of trust. And remember, always accept any and all financial gifts with graciousness and never forget to say thank you!

4 Show and Tell

Community partners want to see their resources in action. That is one of the mistakes some schools make—you can't see the partnership. If you get money from your partners, have a plan to use it quickly. Let them know your intentions for using it and how it will impact all of your scholars. Be thoughtful of how the money will help your school be better. If the partner gave you money for a new library, show pictures of your scholars reading the books in the library. It shows gratitude and your school community can reap the benefits! Remember this game? It was one of my favorites in elementary school. I loved to stand in front of the class and share something I had or bought. It meant

Action Steps

a lot to me to show and tell my class the things that mattered to me. I had this same feeling when it was time for me to show and tell about the progress being made as a result of the community partnership I had with corporations and CEOs. I would show and tell in different formats. Sometimes I would share in company meetings, emails, school newsletters, personal letters, pictures, and even short video clips.

The companies and philanthropic organizations who were in partnership with us loved it! They actually would use that information to share with their teams. They would always be so grateful for me taking the time to do that. I implore you to replicate this. Your community partners want to know if they are making a difference or not.

Be willing to share how their financial contributions were spent with everyone! Tell your scholars, parents, staff, district leaders, and community leaders. Share it through various mediums, such as print, online, and word of mouth.

The worst thing a school can do is to be quiet about their community partnership progress. Now, I get it. Some partners will be confidential or anonymous. That is fine. However, your gift does not need to be. Even anonymous partners want to know they are making an impact that is worthwhile.

5 Be an Investment

While financial gifts are a wonderful thing, you really want more than that! You want community partners to be vested in your mission, vision, and goals. That is deeper than just a check.

As I said earlier, they are looking for good ground to invest in and they want a return as well. Let your partner know your school will be a great investment. A great investment for a corporation means they will get a great return. That return means your scholars will be better educated and have access and opportunities for success.

Community partners want to see that they are a help in what you are doing and that progress is being made. Find ways to show them that their investment is impacting your scholars!

Many of your community partners have a board of directors and other investors who need to be updated on any financial contributions or partnerships they are involved in. By keeping them in the loop, you can prove that the investment they made in your school was worth every cent. That's all the return they need!

6 Know the Financial Terrain

Before you start reaching out to community partners for money, it is wise to familiarize yourself with the financial terrain. Every district has a process for accepting financial gifts, and you need to know what yours is. The worst thing you can do is get a check and not know what to do with it.

So take a day to make an appointment with your district's accounting department manager so you can learn about the correct process. Build a relationship with this person and let him or her know you plan on receiving more and more financial contributions and need to know the rules around accepting such contributions.

There are some districts that are not used to receiving financial gifts for schools and they may be a bit rusty on this, but you can be the school that is the model for the rest to follow. Whatever your district's process is, all financial gifts from community partners have to be acknowledged and approved by your school board. Keeping good records and working closely with your accounting department will help you tremendously and keep a clean trail.

The district may even provide general thank-you letters and receipts to the partner who made the donation. I remember this happened in my

Action Steps

district when I was at the school that began receiving large numbers of financial gifts. My school district accounting representative and I had a system. Once I received a check, I would quickly hand it over to them, they would list it on our school board agenda, they would provide a receipt and thank-you letters, and they would update our school community partnership budget. It was awesome! I must say, we had to get to this point together because my school was the only school continuously receiving financial gifts.

You can learn a lot from the district representatives. All districts are happy to see schools gain community partnerships and increase lines of funding, but they want you to do it correctly. There are guidelines and you have to abide by them, no matter how excited you are.

I had to remember that the school was not mine and that it belonged to the district. That means they are partly responsible for my actions in terms of my relationships with community partners. The same is true for you. That thought alone should make you even more cautious and careful when handling financial contributions. This is not to scare you, but to educate you so you can get it right!

7 Seek Longevity and Sustainability

Financial support for your school can last a long time. I know this, because I have had some community partners who have given to my school for over 10 years, such as WME, Lawry's The Prime Rib restaurant, and many more!

These partners became friends and their work was sustainable. That means they literally became part of the fabric of our school. Their financial contribution was not a one-time event. It was not here today and gone tomorrow. We planned year after year on how to reach our goals, set targets, and fund opportunities that we could not do alone.

Having a sustainable partner requires developing a relationship and including them in your planning. I would actually invite my community partners to our goal-setting meeting and budget reviews. I was surprised at how much input, expertise, and ideas they had for sustaining our partnership and opportunities for the youth we all served.

This was really the reason our partners were our partners for so long. I can tell you they are partners with me even today because our focus was always sustainability to see great things happen for our youth. You can do the same and have many long-lasting partnerships.

8 Steer Clear of the Traps

Yes, there are some traps, some obvious and some not so obvious. I have listed some here based upon my experiences and the experiences of other principals who shared the traps they fell into. So here are some that may help you:

- Never take a personal check, no matter how good it looks. By accepting cashier's checks, your bank will be your backup. Whether you believe this or not, "school" is a business and it must treated as one. There are checks and balances that must be in place. When you begin accepting financial support, you are in the business of schooling. Always make a copy of any check you receive from a community partner before you hand it over to your school district. They could lose it, misplace it, or deposit it in the wrong account. It happens! It's called human error. Don't hold onto cashier's checks. Have a sense of urgency and get them to your district account representative. I remember driving fast to the district to turn in checks before they closed. It was necessary because I never wanted to accidentally lose or misplace them.

- Never accept cash. This is a big no-no! It may be tempting, but cash can't be tracked and is largely frowned upon.

- Always keep a "community partnership" file so you can keep copies of checks, letters, receipts, and anything else connected to the financial contributions. You never know when you will need to refer back to it.

- Never deposit any funds into your personal account. I know this is an obvious trap, but you would be surprised at how many people do this. Look, you don't want to wear an orange jumpsuit, do you? I know I didn't. Over the years, I have heard many good reasons. They did it so they would not leave it at the school, or they wanted to make sure it got cashed because the district process is too slow. All of those reasons are understandable, even if not condoned. However, people, don't do it! It is not worth it! The implications and perceptions of that are bad. Yes, school districts may be notoriously slow because there is a process and bureaucracy for this kind of thing. So let your partners know this so they understand it may take 30 to 60 days. It may be shorter, but they need to know the pace of most school districts. They will understand and thank you for it.

- Be careful about announcing how much money you received. I can remember making a morning announcement about our new computers we had that were purchased for us. The next week, we had a break-in. I know it was because of my enthusiasm and lack of good judgment.

9 Curb Your Enthusiasm

Sometimes we can get too excited and find ourselves either using the money up or spending it without a plan. Don't spend any money before you get it. This happened to a principal I know who ordered tickets to an event for her students and the funds never came through. Then she had to pay for it out of the district's budget, which they did not plan for. Wait until the money is approved and deposited.

10 Follow the Money

Watch your money once you hand it over to the district. If you have a budget, ask for it. Make sure they put it in the right account and that it is not being used for something else without your consent. While your school belongs to the district, the funds must and should be used for what they were intended for. You can lose a partner if the district somehow uses the funds for something they feel is more important. You should make this very clear with your accounting representative as well. If the money goes into your districts' general fund, you might as well say goodbye to it. This is not your PTA or school council budget. Those are separate and different. Be careful, because a lot of money brings a lot of attention. Build a community partnership team to help you spend the money. Never do this alone. You can cause animosity and unneeded speculation about the financial contribution even if you are spending it correctly.

 FURTHERING THE CONVERSATION

Schools Cannot Do It Alone: Building Public Support for America's Public Schools by Jamie Vollmer

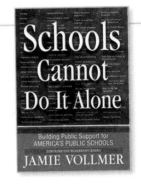

No generation of educators in history has been asked to do what Americans now demand of their public schools. Each year the burden grows, and each day millions of teachers and administrators give everything they've got to meet the challenge. Their record of achievement is remarkable. But no matter how hard they work, or how often they are criticized, they cannot produce the results our nation needs. Not because they are arrogant, overpaid, or unionized but because America's educators cannot "teach all children to high levels" because they work in a system designed to do something else: select and sort young people for an industrial society that no longer exists.

Schools Cannot Do It Alone tells of Jamie Vollmer's extraordinary journey through the land of public education. His experiences led him to two critical discoveries. First, we have a systems problem, not a people problem. We must change the system to get the graduates we need. Second, we cannot touch the system without touching the culture of the surrounding town; everything that goes on inside a school is tied to local attitudes, values, traditions, and beliefs. Drawing on his work in hundreds of districts, Jamie offers teachers, administrators, board members, and their allies a practical program to secure the understanding, trust, permission, and support they need to change the system and increase student success.

Finally, manage your funds and use the money in the way that your community partner intended. It will be tempting when other needs are right in front of you. Don't do it! If they gave you money to purchase soccer uniforms, don't use it for new classroom rugs to be placed in your kindergarten classrooms.

Take the Why Not? Challenge: Look at Your Financial Needs

Make an appointment with your school district's accounting manager to discuss your community partnership goals and how to navigate the terrain of financial gift donations. Take notes and ask a lot of questions. Create a file called "Community Partnerships" so you can be ready to place copies of items in there. Create a relationship with your accounting team and get ready to open the gates to new funding streams that will create opportunities and access for your school.

 REFLECTION PROMPTS

- **Whom do you know in your district's accounting department?**
- **Why is your school a good financial investment for a potential community partner?**
- **What other traps can you think of that you can avoid?**
- **Do you know the cost of some of the things your school wants or needs?**
- **What can you do to sustain some of your existing partners?**
- **Who needs to be on your community partnership team?**

Avoid Partnership Pitfalls

Yes, there are some pitfalls along the road of community empowerment. I have learned many lessons along the way that I would like to share with you as you develop partnerships for your school. As I have said before, this is hard work. While it reaps many benefits, there are some pitfalls you must be aware of.

As I have worked with many schools, I have seen educators and partners alike make mistakes that have caused their good work

to be less than effective and even distracting. This is why it is absolutely important to know why you want to partner and for what purpose. Without that moral compass, your partnership will not be well received among others who will be involved. Let me share a few examples.

One principal brought on a wonderful robotics/STEM partner for the entire school but failed to fully explain the partnership with the staff. This caused confusion and division among the team because they worked with some classes and not with others. Another principal failed to link the partnership to learning. Instead of the partnership supporting what the school was doing academically, it actually took away from their learning, causing test scores to decline. It wasn't because it was not a good partnership, it was because it was not supporting what they were doing in the classroom, thereby causing a conflict. The partner should have been included in the professional development and in collaboration with the teachers to create alignment. Finally, another principal did not create a team for sustainable community partnerships. She wanted to do the work all by herself. This kept the partner waiting many times because there was no one else assigned to be the contact person besides the principal. Running a school is hard enough, but to keep up with the partnership as well is almost impossible. She needed a team around her who could collaborate with her about the partnership and its purpose. She also needed to identify key contact individuals who could be accessible and respond to the partner's needs. A team would have really helped her and the success of the partnership.

> **66** *It is absolutely important to know why you want to partner and for what purpose. Without that moral compass, your partnership will not be well received.* **99**

These were pitfalls that caused each partner to either slow down and, in some cases, cease. That is not what you want! In this chapter, I want you to learn from each pitfall that I personally experienced or saw other educational leaders experience.

Action Steps for Avoiding Partnership Pitfalls

1 Engage Your Team With Partnership Selections

Seek input from your team. Not fully including your team about potential partners or asking for their ideas may result in confusion and lack of effective teamwork. Seek input from your team so they can be engaged in the process. This will help create better relationships that need to be formed when the partner arrives. As a team, you can share ideas about how to match and align the partner with your learning goals.

2 Follow Protocol

Safety first! Make sure your partnership goes through the legal process to be on campus with your scholars. Usually there is a school board approval process that just can't be rushed. Inform your partner of the waiting period and follow the guidelines your district has in place. Don't allow any partnership to start before this process has fully gone through. There is a process of vetting, background checks, fingerprints, and even more before a partnership can officially begin. If you move too quickly, you could get in trouble for not following the rules and the partnership could be terminated. Remember, the school belongs to the district and you are the overseer of the school and the scholars in your care. It is important for you to be astute about that process so you can prepare your partner and your staff.

3 Identify a Contact Person

Identifying a contact person for the partnership has saved me every time! In the beginning, I was the contact person, which took a toll. My busy schedule kept them waiting on me to return calls and I sometimes missed appointments, which was embarrassing. This can create miscommunication and chaos for everyone. I started asking volunteers, teachers, or office clerks to assist me. By engaging people other than yourself for this role, you will be more organized and it will build capacity among your team. The contact person might be another administrator, lead teacher, main office person, or a parent volunteer. Just make sure he or she is trained about the details of the partnership. The whole purpose is to create a flow of conversation, good relationships, and a successful partnership. If you pick the wrong person to be your contact, you could easily jeopardize the partnership before it even begins. Think about it, seek volunteers, and make sure it is a good match.

4 Put Some Skin in the Game

Please don't expect the partner to do all the work! Unfortunately, I have seen this example happen more times than I wanted to. The partner comes with great opportunities and resources and the school is the receiver. While your partner will come with resources that you will love, he or she is also in partnership with you and the work needs to be equal to be successful. This means work on your side. Your partner knows how busy you are, but there are some things only we can do to help the partnership work. Here are some things to keep in mind: pre-planning any logistics for activities; showing up at scheduled meetings; being present at partnership events, and/or sending a representative; helping him or her organize any activities and following up with your team to

make sure everything goes off smoothly; communicating events with your stakeholders; promoting events; creating flyers, etc. Your attention to that kind of detail is monumental so no one's time is wasted. You want to show your partner that you bring value to the table as well.

5 Monitor and Evaluate Your Partnership

One of my former superintendents used to say, "If you don't inspect it, don't expect it." If you expect any partnership to be successful, check in on it often and see how you can help. Look for the patterns and gaps. Just like every program or initiative on your campus, every partnership needs monitoring and evaluating. Go by and check on any partnership activities that may be happening on a given day. Your presence will mean a lot! Add those visits to your regular classroom visits. See the partnership as a part of the fabric of your school—not an addition. If you don't, the partner could feel unsupported and may not want to continue working with your school. Listen to the end users. Your teachers, scholars, parents, and custodians will give you good insight into what is happening when you are not around. Take time to listen to your entire staff who are working directly with your partner. You want to consider their thoughts and ideas for any improvements and they will appreciate that! Also, don't forget to meet with your partner on a regular basis and ask them how the partnership is going. They will be able to help shape the context and share what worked or didn't for them. I suggest doing this quarterly so you can make changes as needed. You can use surveys, questionnaires, and have check-in meetings. All of those will provide you with data on how to avoid any pitfalls.

6 Keep Learning as the Focus

While the partnership is great, don't forget the reason you reached out to develop partners in the first place. It was to support the learning and academic achievement for your scholars. That's it! If you can keep that as the focus, then everything else will be done well because that was your overall intention. DuFour, DuFour, and Eaker (2008) assert that the first big idea of a professional learning community is a focus on learning. I admit, sometimes it's easy to get sidetracked and lose focus. When you keep your scholars and learning as the focus, it will help guide every partnership decision you make. I suggest reviewing your goals monthly with your team and inviting your partners in that conversation. This will create common language, alignment, and focus. It will also reduce pitfalls.

 FURTHERING THE CONVERSATION

Cultural Competence Now: 56 Exercises to Help Educators Understand and Challenge Bias, Racism, and Privilege
by Vernita Mayfield

What will it take to create equitable educational opportunities for all students? According to veteran educator Vernita Mayfield, teachers and school leaders need to learn how to recognize culturally embedded narratives about racial hierarchy and dismantle the systems of privilege and the institutions that perpetuate them with knowledge, action, and advocacy.

Cultural Competence Now provides a structure to begin meaningful conversations about race, culture, bias, privilege, and power within the time constraints of an ordinary school. The 56 exercises include activities, discussions, and readings in which to engage during each of the four quarters of the school year. School leaders will discover how to facilitate learning through the four steps—1) awaken and assess; 2) apply and act; 3) analyze and align; 4) advocate and lead.

Mayfield offers advice on establishing a safe environment for professional conversations, setting goals for cultural competency, overcoming resistance, reviewing school data and the school's vision and mission through the lens of race and culture, and strategically managing what can be a transformative yet uncomfortable change process. *Cultural Competence Now* responds to the urgent need to build the cultural competency of educators—for the sake of children and in the interest of supporting and retaining all educators.

Take the Why Not? Challenge: Evaluate Your Partnership Program

Schedule time on your calendar to monitor and/or evaluate your partnership program. By putting it on your calendar and sharing with your team, you will have included an excellent managerial step toward checks and balances of a great partnership.

 REFLECTION PROMPTS

- Which one of the action steps resonated with you and why?
- If you could pick one of them to do better, which one would you choose?
- Which one are you excelling at?
- Who will be your contact person for your partnership?
- How can you tweak how you monitor or evaluate your partnership programs?

References

Barth, R. (1991). Restructuring schools: Some questions for teachers and principals. *Phi Delta Kappan, 73*(2), 123–129.

Blank, M., Jacobson, R., Melaville, A., & Pearson, S. (2010). *Financing community schools: Leveraging resources to support student success.* Washington, DC: Coalition for Community Schools, Institute for Educational Leadership.

Carey, G. W., & Frohnen, B. (1998). *Community and tradition: Conservative perspectives on the American experience.* Lanham, MD: Rowman & Littlefield Publishers.

Chadwick, K. G. (2003). *Improving schools through community engagement: A practical guide for educators.* Thousand Oaks, CA: Corwin.

Cuban, L. (1998, January 28). A tale of two schools. *Education Week, 17*(20).

DuFour, R., & Eaker, R. (1998). *Professional learning communities at work: Best practices for enhancing student achievement.* Bloomington, IN: National Educational Service.

DuFour, R., DuFour, R., & Eaker, R. (2008). *Revisiting professional learning communities at work: New insights for improving schools.* Bloomington, IN: Solution Tree Press.

Dweck, C. S. (2007). *Mindset: The new psychology of success.* New York: Ballantine Books.

Epstein, J. L., & Associates. (2008). *School, family, and community partnerships: Your handbook for action, third edition.* Thousand Oaks, CA: Corwin.

Eury, A. D. (2018). Equity in schools: What administrators need to know. TeachHub. Retrieved from: https://www.teachhub.com/equity-schools-what-administrators-need-know

Gabriel, J. G., & Farmer, P. C. (2009). *How to help your school thrive without breaking the bank.* Alexandria, VA: ASCD.

Glasser, W. (1998). *Choice theory: A new psychology of personal freedom.* New York: HarperCollins Publishers.

Hallam, S. (2010). The power of music: Its impact on the intellectual, social and personal development of children and young people. *International Journal of Music Education, 28*(3), 269–289.

Henderson, R. M. (2018, February 12). More and more CEOs are taking their social responsibility seriously. *Harvard Business Review.* Retrieved from: https://hbr.org/2018/02/more-and-more-ceos-are-taking-their-social-responsibility-seriously

Hill, P., Foster, G., & Gendler, T. (1990). *High schools with character.* Santa Monica: The RAND Corporation.

Kouzes, J. M., & Posner, B. Z. (2017). *The leadership challenge: How to make extraordinary things happen in organizations, sixth edition.* San Francisco, CA: Jossey Bass.

Mapp, K., Carver, I., & Lander, J. (2017). *Powerful partnerships: A teacher's guide to engaging families for student success.* New York: Scholastic.

Marzano, R. J., Pickering, D. J., & Pollock, J. E. (2001). *Classroom instruction that works: Research-based strategies for increasing student achievement.* Alexandria, VA: ASCD.

Mayfield, V. (2020). *Cultural competence now: 56 exercises to help educators understand and challenge bias, racism, and privilege.* Alexandria, VA: ASCD.

Price, H. B. (2008). *Mobilizing the community to help students succeed.* Alexandria, VA: ASCD.

Ripp, P. S. (2014). *Empowered schools, empowered students: Creating connected and invested learners.* Thousand Oaks, CA: Corwin.

Ruppert, S. S. (2009). Why schools with arts programs do better at narrowing achievement gaps. *Education Week, 29*(5).

Schellenberg, E. G. (2004). Music lessons enhance IQ. *Psychological Science, 15*(8), 511–514.

Schellenberg, E. G. (2006). Long-term positive associations between music lessons and IQ. *Journal of Educational Psychology, 98*(2), 457.

Sinek, S., Mead, D., & Docker, P. (2017). *Find your why: A practical guide for discovering purpose for you and your team.* New York: Portfolio.

Taylor, B. (2016). "Awakening Corporate America." APB Speaker Series. Retrieved from: https://www.youtube.com/watch?v=wxp13vgRcUM

Taylor, R., & Chanter, C. (2019). *The coaching partnership: Collaboration for systemic change.* New York: Scholastic.

Tichy, N. M. (1997). *Transformational leader: The key to global competitiveness.* Hoboken, NJ: Wiley.

Vollmer, J. (2010). *Schools cannot do it alone: Building public support for American's public schools.* New York: Enlightenment Press.

Index